METHODOLOGY IN THE SOCIAL SCIENCES
David A. Kenny, *Series Editor*

PRINCIPLES AND PRACTICE OF
STRUCTURAL EQUATION MODELING
Rex B. Kline

SPECTRAL ANALYSIS OF
TIME-SERIES DATA
Rebecca M. Warner

A PRIMER ON REGRESSION ARTIFACTS
Donald T. Campbell and David A. Kenny

A Primer on
REGRESSION ARTIFACTS

DONALD T. CAMPBELL
DAVID A. KENNY

Foreword by Charles S. Reichardt

THE GUILFORD PRESS
New York   London

© 1999 The Guilford Press
A Division of Guilford Publications, Inc.
72 Spring Street, New York, NY 10012
http://www. guilford.com

Printed in the United States of America

This book is printed on acid-free paper.

Last digit is print number: 9   8   7   6   5   4   3   2   1

Library of Congress Cataloging-in-Publication Data

Campbell, Donald Thomas, 1916–1996
    A primer on regression artifacts / Donald T. Campbell and David A. Kenny.
        p.   cm. — (Methodology in the social sciences)
    Includes bibliographical references and index.
    ISBN 1-57230-482-0
    1. Regression analysis.   2. Social sciences—Statistical methods.
    I. Kenny, David A., 1946–   . II. Title.   III. Series.
    HA31.3.C35   1999
    519.5'36—DC21   99-23003
                                                            CIP

To those who worked with Donald T. Campbell;
may they continue to make science timeless!

About the Authors

Donald T. Campbell, PhD, before his death in 1996 was University Professor of Social Relations, Psychology, and Education at Lehigh University. He had previously taught at Ohio State University, the University of Chicago, Northwestern University, and Syracuse University. He was a member of the National Academy of Sciences and a President of the American Psychological Association. He was the recipient of nine honorary doctorates.

David A. Kenny, PhD, is Professor of Social Psychology at the University of Connecticut. He has been a visiting professor at Oxford University and Arizona State University. He was a Fellow at the Center for Advanced Study in the Behavioral Sciences.

Foreword

Regression toward the mean is as inevitable as death and taxes. Academic performance, emotional well-being, medical diagnosis, investment return, athletic feats, motion picture sales, and any other variables you can think of all exhibit regression toward the mean. But even more remarkable than the ubiquitousness of regression toward the mean is how commonly the phenomenon is misunderstood, usually with undesirable consequences. Social scientists incorrectly estimate the effects of ameliorative interventions, sports writers misguidedly attribute poor performance to jinxes, and snake-oil peddlers earn a healthy living all because our intuition fails when trying to comprehend regression toward the mean. Even intellectual prowess is not an antidote to this shortcoming. Sir Francis Galton is one of those rare geniuses whose name is still renowned 90 years after his death. This is, in part, because Galton was the first to recognize and provide a label for "regression toward mediocrity." Galton even demonstrated convincingly that individual height regresses to the mean across generations. But he got it wrong when he tried to explain how regression toward the mean operates.

If someone of Galton's immense intellectual abilities cannot understand regression toward the mean even when looking it square in the eye, how can we mere mortals expect to figure it out? The answer is, in more ways than one, within your grasp. The elegant and concise volume you hold in your hands provides a simple and comprehensive explanation. This is not to say that understanding the volume's content will always be easy. The mystery of regression toward the mean is not going to be revealed without effort on your part. You must be willing to grapple at times with no-tions that appear to violate common sense. You must be prepared to stop on occasion to puzzle over apparent paradoxes. But if you are willing to extend yourself just a little, your efforts will be well rewarded. If you are a novice in the topic, you will become an expert by reading A *Primer on Regression Artifacts*. If you are already an expert, you will learn things you will be surprised you did not already know. In either case, you will find that the authors meet you more than halfway; they guide your inquiry with ample encouragement, engaging illustrations, and good humor. As a result, your reading will prove to be both eye-opening and enjoyable.

Of course, those in the know would expect no less from Don Campbell and Dave Kenny. They are two of the preeminent social science methodologists of our generation. It is hard to imagine a duo that is more capable of making comprehensible a challenging methodological topic.

Under ordinary circumstances, no more need be said about either of the authors because of their stellar reputations. But circumstances are not ordinary and a few more words must be said about Campbell in particular. There are few, if any, scholars who have had as sustained and profound an influence on research methods in the social sciences as Campbell has had. For example, Campbell's separate volumes on quasi-experimentation with Julian Stanley and with Tom Cook are the equivalent of the old and the new testaments of research design. Campbell's article with Don Fiske on the multitrait–multimethod matrix is the single most widely cited article in the *Psychological Bulletin* in the last 50 years. Based on such work, Campbell has received virtually every honor that is available to a research psychologist. If the Nobel prize were awarded in psychology, he would likely have won that as well. As a result, Campbell's name, like Galton's, will be revered long after his death. Sadly, that time period has already begun, for Don Campbell died in the spring of 1996.

Campbell and Kenny planned the present volume together, and they wrote much of it together before Don's untimely death. But Kenny had to finish it alone. The result is a tribute to Kenny's dedication both to Don and to the topic of regression toward the mean. Kenny has done both of them proud.

While Campbell was passionate about all of his work, there was no topic he embraced with more fervor than regression toward the mean. He never tired of talking about it, and he very much wanted others to come to understand it as he did. As a result, Don is now smiling. He has seen the publication of the last, and one of the most beloved, of his works.

By now Don has also, I am sure, tracked down Sir Francis and the two of them have had many enlivened chats about regression toward the mean. If you turn the page, you can listen in on that conversation. I know Campbell would be delighted to have you join him. Don was one of those special individuals who loved everyone he met and who loved to talk to them about science. We owe Dave Kenny a tremendous debt of gratitude for so well bringing to fruition this opportunity for one last visit with Don and the ideas he cherished.

CHARLES S. REICHARDT
University of Denver

Preface

Regression toward the mean is an artifact that as easily fools statistical experts as lay people. The universal phenomenon of regression toward the mean is just as universally misunderstood. Regression toward the mean is a very subtle phenomenon and easy to miss. This primer is replete with examples of how it is overlooked in everyday life as well as in statistical analysis. Our purpose is to increase understanding and comprehension of this concept.

One reason we decided to write this primer now is that much of the recent work on research methodology has downplayed or ignored the importance of regression toward the mean. For instance, the recent edited book on *Best Methods for the Analysis of Change* (Collins & Horn, 1991) does not even include the entry of "regression toward the mean" in its index. Some have even argued that regression toward the mean is an overrated problem (Gottman & Rushe, 1993). We were motivated to write this primer because the classic contributions by F. M. Lord, Q. McNemar, L. J. Cronbach, L. Furby, and L. G. Humphreys as well as the large body of work by the first author (Campbell & Boruch, 1975; Campbell & Clayton, 1961; Campbell & Erlebacher, 1970; Campbell & Stanley, 1963; Cook & Campbell, 1979) are being ignored.

Regression toward the mean can be approached from many points of view: statistics, cognitive psychology, psychometrics, evaluation research, and biology. We will throughout this primer look at the concept through these different lenses. We have chosen to concentrate on the effects of regression toward the mean on the measurement of change in program evaluation research because it is the area in which we have worked in the past. We realize that regression toward the mean applies much more broadly than change

(Lund, 1989a), but we feel that many of misunderstandings of the concept are located in this one area.

Our emphasis in this primer is on the problem of regression toward the mean in scores measured two or more times. Thus, we consider issues in the analysis of longitudinal and time-series data. A related emphasis in the primer is that very often we are interested in evaluating the effect of a treatment or intervention. We believe that mistaken conclusions in treatment evaluations sometimes occur because of a failure to understand regression toward the mean. As shown in this primer, ironically it is sometimes the "correction" for regression toward the mean that creates the problem.

In the first and most important chapter, we describe the phenomenon of regression toward the mean in a nontechnical fashion. We avoid presenting formulas but instead focus on a graphical presentation. The emphasis is on the conceptual and not the mathematical. The more knowledgeable readers may be tempted to skip this chapter, but we strongly encourage them not to do so, as it presents the perfect-correlation line, the pair-link diagram, and the Galton squeeze diagram; all of these new concepts are featured throughout this primer.

In Chapter 2, we present the mathematics of regression toward the mean and answer some commonly asked questions about the concept. We also generalize regression toward the mean beyond the simplifications of the first chapter. Although this chapter is more mathematical than the first, we still heavily rely on graphical methods.

The next seven chapters consider regression artifacts, the focus of the primer. However, Chapters 6 and 9 do not concern quasi-experimental evaluations, and so some may wish to skip those chapters. In Chapter 3, we show that when a group of persons are measured over time, their average score regresses toward the mean. This chapter presents several illustrations of regression toward the mean in everyday life, including the so-called sophomore jinx in baseball. It also considers the often-ignored problem of misclassification caused by regression toward the mean.

Chapters 4 and 5 consider regression toward the mean in the nonequivalent control group design. In Chapter 4, we show that matching of scores on a variable only partially controls for group differences. Chapter 5 shows that statistical equating (methods that covary out the pretest) is usually not totally successful.

Chapter 6 focuses on the measurement of change and describes regression artifacts in change score analysis. There is no intervention; we are just trying to identify who changed more. We learn that change is a much more difficult topic than might be thought.

The next three chapters consider regression artifacts in more complicated situations. Chapter 7 considers regression toward the mean in time-series research, and Chapter 8 considers longitudinal research. For both of these topics we present several examples. In Chapter 9, we review the technique of cross-lagged panel correlation and discuss its potential uses.

Finally, in Chapter 10, several common themes are reiterated. These themes include the utility of time-reversed analysis, graphical presentation of raw data, the importance of design in research, and the consideration of plausible rival hypotheses. We also discuss how forecasters and prognosticators often fail to take into account regression toward the mean.

We realize that readers have varying backgrounds. We assume that all readers have had at least one course in statistics and research design. We presume some knowledge of significance testing, random assignment and selection, reliability, and correlation. Moreover, we assume some knowledge about the classical threats to validity that were developed by Campbell and Stanley (1963). We do occasionally discuss more advanced topics for which complete comprehension requires knowledge of multiple regression, time-series analysis, structural equation modeling, or multilevel modeling. Even when these topics are discussed, we attempt to present them in as nontechnical a fashion as possible. A Glossary of Terms is included at the end of this primer so that the reader can study definitions of new concepts. Issues of significance testing are downplayed, and more emphasis is given to estimation of intervention effects.

We have tried to reduce the number of formulas in this primer, and so we have avoided presenting formulas for statistics that are commonly given in standard texts. Chapter 6, the measurement of change, has many formulas because many such formulas have been proposed. Most of the other formulas that we have presented are for the amount of regression toward the mean expected under different circumstances. The formulas are not complex and are simple variants of the standard regression prediction equation.

When faced with decisions about how much complexity to allow in our discussions, simulations, and formulas, we have tried to opt for the simplest possible model. We have oversimplified the cases that we are discussing, but we do so to sharpen the focus on the central topic of this primer: regression toward the mean.

*   *   *

The contents of this primer are part of the extraordinary legacy of Donald T. Campbell. Tragically, he died in the middle of this project. Although he made numerous contributions to many fields, he believed that his work on regression toward the mean was one of his most important methodological contributions. To quote from one of his last papers: "I find myself the most fanatic teacher of the problem of regression artifacts . . . and I recommend continued attention to this problem" (Campbell, 1994, p. 294).

Don Campbell had many collaborators who worked with him or who took his ideas on regression toward the mean and worked on their own. Among them were Robert F. Boruch, Keith N. Clayton, Thomas D. Cook, Albert Erlebacher, William M. Trochim, and Charles S. Reichardt. Many of their contributions are represented in this primer, and so they should be considered as unnamed coauthors.

In making changes in the manuscript after Campbell's death, I have tried to remain faithful to his point of view. Despite my efforts, I cannot begin to match the creativity and genius that would have been evident had he been able to make the final revisions. I do worry that there may have been times that I wrote "we" in this primer and Campbell may not have agreed with such conclusions. This was a particular concern in Chapters 6, 9, and 10, which were entirely written after his death. I have attempted, as best I could, to represent his views fairly (and I have asked his past colleagues if I have done so). I also know, having written several papers with him, that he was very trusting of his coauthors. I have diligently tried to finish writing this book as Don would have wanted it. Knowing Don, he would have liked, and even been proud of, the final product but would never have allowed himself to be the first author.

A strong debt of gratitude is due to the many who have helped us in this project. Thanks are due to Brian Lashley and Virginia Carrow, who assisted in the preparation of this primer. Katherine Kenny guided the production and prepared many of the figures. I also wish to thank Deborah Kashy, Andrea Piccinin, Thomas Malloy, Lynn Winquist, Cynthia Mohr, Lee Cronbach, and Dale Griffin, who provided me with feedback. I want especially to thank Charles M. Judd, Charles S. Reichardt, and Dale Griffin, whose input led to many major changes in the primer. These colleagues often challenged me and provoked me to think in new ways. Their suggestions considerably improved the presentation. Also helpful were presentations given by me at the University of Geneva and the University of Kansas. Patrick Quinn, the archivist of the Northwestern University library, kindly gave me access to Don Campbell's materials. Finally, I thank Barbara Frankel, Campbell's widow, who has assisted me in countless ways throughout this entire project.

DAVID A. KENNY
Storrs, Connecticut

Contents

The Importance of Research Design, 164
Careful Consideration of Plausible Rival Hypotheses, 165
Regression and Prediction, 167
Conclusion, 170

1

Graphical Introduction

Consider the following phenomena:

Many parents think that punishment improves bad behavior and that rewards do not sustain good behavior (Kahneman & Tversky, 1973).

Rookies of the year in major league baseball seem to suffer from a sophomore jinx (Taylor & Cuave, 1994).

Some children assigned to remedial programs do not seem to belong in such programs.

Some very depressed people spontaneously become much less depressed.

The sequel to a movie is usually not as good as the original movie.

High school students who do poorly on their Scholastic Aptitude Tests (SATs) seem to improve remarkably after taking an SAT preparation course.

These and many other phenomena can be explained by regression toward the mean. The universal phenomenon of regression toward the mean is universally misunderstood. It is a very subtle phenomenon and easy to miss. This primer is replete with examples of how it is overlooked in everyday life by lay people as well as in statistical analyses by experts. The purpose of this primer is to increase understanding and comprehension of this difficult concept.

In this introductory chapter, we present a nontechnical, largely graphical description of regression toward the mean. We emphasize graphical over algebraic presentation. (The algebra is deferred until the next chapter.) We urge readers to follow the discussion in

1

the text by creating their own data and drawing their own figures. A computer program described in Appendix A can reproduce the figures in this chapter. We encourage the reader to access this computer program.

The chapter contains many new terms, all of which are repeatedly defined and illustrated. However, readers can refer to the Glossary of Terms in the back of the primer to refresh their memories.

To begin to understand the concept of regression toward the mean, consider a group of students who take two examinations. The essential fact of regression toward the mean can be communicated in terms of ranks. The student who ranked number one on the first exam will almost certainly not rank as high on the second exam, evidencing a loss in rank. But the student who ranked number one on the second exam will almost certainly have improved in status since the first. Comparably, the student ranking lowest at the first exam will probably not rank lowest on the second exam and the student ranking lowest on the second exam will probably not rank lowest on the first. The fact that performance declines for those who do the best and improves for those have done the worst is an inherent feature of change that has confused and perplexed researchers for more than 100 years.

The first data analyst to be fooled by regression artifacts was the person who named it, Sir Francis Galton. In the late 1800s, he measured the height of 928 children[1] and their parents. To make female heights equivalent to male heights, he multiplied them by 1.08. Galton (1886) noticed that tall parents tended to have tall children, but the children were not quite as tall as their parents, something he called "filial regression toward mediocrity" (p. 246). So, for instance, if the parent was 70.5 inches tall, the child tended to be 69.5 inches in height. Galton also noticed that short parents tended to have short children, but again the children were not quite as short as their parents. So, for instance, if the parents were 65.5 inches in height, their children were on average about 66.7 inches tall. He reasoned that there must be some sort of biological force that made people move toward the mean, and he called that force *regression* (Galton, 1879, 1886). Galton eventually realized

---

[1]In the text of his paper, Galton (1886) stated that there were 930 cases; however, his Table I includes only 928 cases. Moreover, it is a curious fact that almost always Galton is cited as showing that "tall fathers have shorter sons." Our use of daughters and mothers is not due to political correctness but rather because Galton used mothers, fathers, sons, and daughters.

that regression was not a biological force but an inherent feature of change. This realization came about by the counterintuitive step of noting that tall children had shorter parents and short children had taller parents. It was difficult to believe that the biological process of regression operated backward in time.

In this chapter, we explain in nontechnical terms and without any formulas what regression toward the mean is and how to recognize it. We adopt Galton's fundamental insight of looking backward in time.

FROM THE SCATTER PLOT TO THE CORRELATION COEFFICIENT

Regression toward the mean occurs whenever two variables are imperfectly related. However, it is helpful to illustrate it when the same variable is measured at two times. Later, in Chapter 2, we consider other applications. To explain the concept of regression toward the mean, we use data based on dice rolls.[2] A roll of one die yields a number from 1 to 6. We encourage readers to roll their own dice and generate their own data set.[3]

To begin, two scores, a pretest and a posttest, are generated. We first roll two dice to get the underlying true score, or T, which will remain the same on both pretest and posttest for each "person." This roll of two dice yields a number from 2 to 12. We then roll two dice for pretest error, E_1, and add this to the true score to get the observed pretest score of X. We now roll two dice for posttest error,[4] or E_2. Next we add this to the true score to get the observed posttest score, or Y. Consider data from one "person." If T equals 8, E_1 equals 12, and E_2 equals 8, then that person's pretest score would be 8 + 12, which equals 20, and the posttest score would be 8 + 8, which equals 16. The sum of four dice yields a number from 4 to 24. This procedure is repeated 20 times. Table 1.1 presents the results of our dice-rolling experiment.

To achieve an intuitive understanding of regression artifacts,

---

[2]Cutter (1976) has shown how dice rolls can be used to illustrate regression toward the mean in the classroom. Levin (1982) proposed a modification using playing cards.

[3]The reader can gain access to the computer program to generate his or her own data set by using the information described in Appendix A.

[4]Classically, errors of measurement have a mean of 0. We take the liberty of having errors with a mean of 7.

TABLE 1.1. 20 Scores from Rolling Four Dice

T	E_1	E_2	X	Y
8	12	8	20	16
9	7	4	16	13
11	7	6	18	17
5	4	7	9	12
6	8	3	14	9
9	6	10	15	19
4	10	4	14	8
11	12	9	23	20
11	11	8	22	19
8	5	5	13	13
7	6	7	13	14
7	9	5	16	12
6	5	2	11	8
2	10	11	12	13
6	7	7	13	13
11	6	10	17	21
9	6	8	15	17
8	10	7	18	15
5	9	5	14	10
5	4	8	9	13

graphical presentations are employed. The typical form used to present a relationship between two variables graphically is the scatter plot or scatter diagram. Most statistics texts only briefly illustrate the scatter plot, but it is featured much more frequently in this primer.

Figure 1.1 shows the results of our dice-rolling simulation as a scatter plot. The horizontal axis (or X-axis) is the pretest or X (the fourth column in Table 1.1). The vertical axis (or Y-axis) represents the posttest or Y (the fifth column in Table 1.1). At each point in the scatter plot where cases occur, we indicate the number of cases at that point. We have circled the plot of the first data point in which the pretest is 20 and the posttest is 16. Note that there are two observations in which the pretest and posttest are both 13.

For those who know what correlation is, the resulting theoretical correlation for the simulation is .5. (It takes on this value because the true score and error are equally weighted; see Appendix A for more details.) However, for the *sample* data in Table 1.1, the correlation coefficient equals .645.

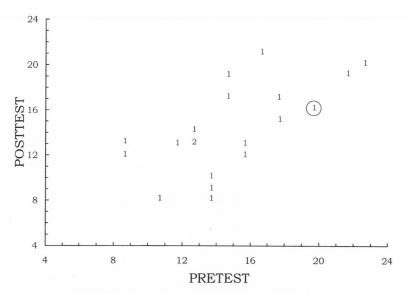

FIGURE 1.1. Scatter plot of the data in Table 1.1.

For the remainder of this section, we shift from the case in Figure 1.1 and Table 1.1 with 20 "persons" to one with 500 "persons." (A procedure for obtaining the data is described in Appendix A.) This large sample size creates more stability for our purely graphical computation of the correlation coefficient. The pretest mean for this larger sample is 14.15, and the posttest mean is 13.96. The standard deviations are 3.50 and 3.57 for the pre- and posttest, respectively. (The theoretical values are 14.00 for the means and 3.42 for the standard deviations.) Figure 1.2 presents the histograms for the pre- and posttest scores before matching. Both distributions show a central peak around 14 and considerable variability.

Figure 1.3 presents the scatter plot for this data set of 500 "persons." For the moment, ignore the boxes around some of the numbers. We adopt the usual convention of presenting numbers in the scatter plot to symbolize the number of points. So, for instance, there are 9 "persons" who scored 12 on both the pretest and the posttest. When there are 10 or more persons at a point in the scatter plot, we use an asterisk (*) as the symbol. The gradual upward trend of the scatter plot indicates that there is a positive association between the pretest and the posttest: as the pretest score increases, the posttest score increases.

Figure 1.4 shows a scatter plot, but instead of plotting all 500

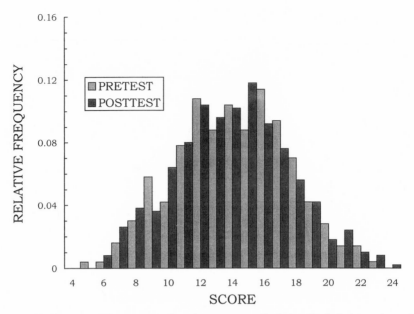

FIGURE 1.2. Histograms for the pretest (lightly shaded boxes) and posttest (darkly shaded boxes) for the data set with 500 "persons."

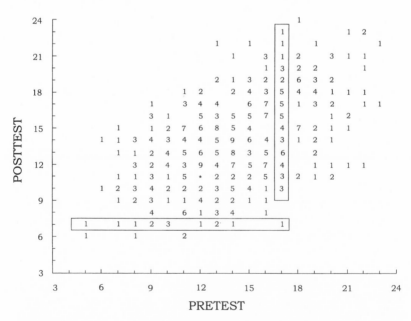

FIGURE 1.3. Scatter plot of 500 "persons" (asterisk indicates 10 or more observations).

6

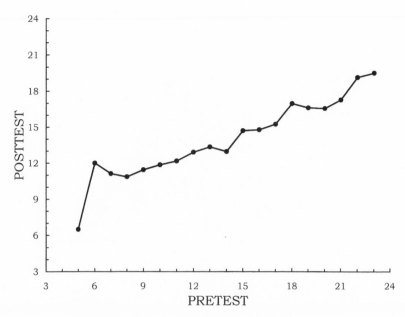

FIGURE 1.4. Vertical squeeze plot of 500 "persons."

pairs of scores, we plot just 20 or so data points. For the moment, let us ignore the lines connecting the points and just concentrate on the dark circles that are the plotted points. For each of the pretest scores for which there are observations available (4 to 24), we have plotted the mean on the posttest. So, for instance, for the score of 10 on the pretest, we plot the posttest mean of all those scoring 10 at the pretest and that mean is 11.86. Thus, the points that are plotted are the posttest means for every pretest score. Because scores are collapsed or squeezed on the vertical or Y-axis, we refer to the type of plot in Figure 1.4 as a *vertical squeeze plot*.

Let us try to understand the rationale of a vertical squeeze plot. Given these 500 data points, what is the best estimate of the posttest score for each pretest score? We consider first those with a pretest score of 23. For these scores, there are only two posttest scores, of 17 and 22. We have very little evidence to go on. But the average of these two posttest scores, 19.5, is a good guess from these sparse data of what a 23 on the pretest will be on the posttest. So, we plot that point on the vertical squeeze plot. For pretest scores of 22, we have more cases, 7 in all. We compute the mean of those 7 scores and get a value of 19.14 for this mean. For pretests of 17, we have drawn a box around the numbers in the scatter plot in Figure 1.3. The mean of those posttest numbers is 15.26. We continue for all values of the pretest.

We now connect the adjacent points in a vertical squeeze plot by a straight line, as is done in Figure 1.4. So we connect the points for pretest scores from 6 to 7, from 7 to 8, and so on. If we had no scores for 5, we would connect the points 4 and 6. The resulting curve is a zigzag line that we call the *overfitted regression line*. Given how the data were generated, the "true" regression line (i.e., the one that we would obtain if we had a very large sample of rolls for each pretest score) would be a perfectly straight line. The overfitted regression line is not perfectly straight because of the finite sample size of pretest scores. (Appendix A describes how a computer program can be downloaded, and the reader can use that program to see how the line straightens as the sample size increases.)

In Figure 1.5, we have taken a transparent ruler and drawn a straight line that best fits the zigzag line (has more or less equal discrepancies above and below the straight line, but with little weight given to discrepancies where there are very few cases). This is the

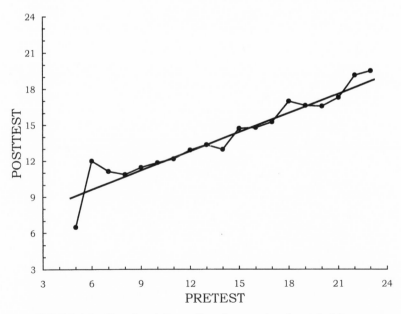

FIGURE 1.5. Overfitted (jagged) and regression (straight) lines.

"guesstimate" regression line, and it is shown in Figure 1.5. Alternatively, the least-squares regression line could be computed using the standard statistical formula presented in most statistics books and it would differ somewhat. However, we are trying to emphasize comprehension in this presentation, not computational precision. We will very frequently just guesstimate and not precisely compute values. By using a guesstimate, we force the reader to look closely at his or her data and not to compute mechanically and mindlessly some abstract statistical quantity. Of course, in scientific reports guesstimates would not be used.

To move from the linear regression line to the correlation coefficient, we need two more lines to which we compare the regression line. These two additional lines are drawn in Figure 1.6 along with the guesstimate regression line. The *perfect-correlation line*, in this situation, would mean that the pretest and the posttest took on the same value. For example, every pretest 22 had a posttest of 22 and every pretest 6 had a posttest of 6. To represent this perfect-correlation line, we draw a straight diagonal line (45 degrees) from

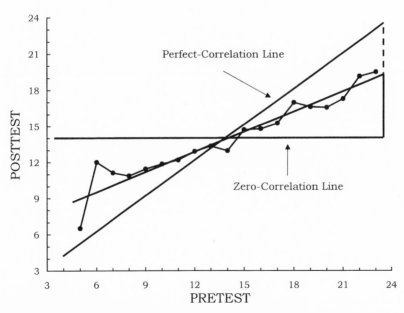

FIGURE 1.6. Perfect (diagonal), zero (flat), and regression (approximately 45-degree) lines; solid vertical line, correlation; dashed vertical line, regression toward the mean.

the upper-right 24–24 point to the lower-left 4–4 point. In Chapter 2, we describe how to draw the perfect-correlation line when the mean and variance change.

We also need to draw in what the regression line would be if the correlation were zero. For a zero correlation, the scatter plot would show a perfectly circular scatter or ball-like structure. A zero correlation implies that knowing the pretest gives us no help at all in predicting the posttest. For each pretest score, the best guess for the posttest is the mean of all posttest scores. The mean of all posttest scores would be 14 if we had rolled enough dice to get rid of sampling errors. (It is 14 because the most likely roll of two dice is 7, and four dice are rolled.) Thus, a posttest score of 14 would be the best prediction for pretest scores of 22 or 6, and for every possible pretest score. To represent this, we draw a horizontal line from a posttest score of 14 on the left vertical axis. Note that the intersection of the perfect-correlation and the guesstimated regression lines fall on the zero-correlation line.

The guesstimate regression line in Figure 1.6 lies about halfway between the perfect-correlation and zero-correlation lines, and so the correlation coefficient is about .50. To get a more precise number, we draw a vertical line on the right side of the figure. For instance, in Figure 1.6 we drew the vertical line at the pretest value of 24. We extend the line from the zero-correlation line to the perfect-correlation line. The total distance of this line (the solid plus the dashed vertical line) is 10 points (i.e., 24 − 14). The guesstimate line is about 5.5 points above the zero-correlation line (the solid line) and is thus 5.5/10 of the way to perfection, and 5.5 divided by 10 equals .55, a guess of what the correlation coefficient is for this data set. Use your own value for the regression line; you will not get exactly the same value, but you should get something close to .5. The actual correlation computed by the conventional formula is .525, not all that far from the .55 value that we obtained by guesstimation.

In general, the correlation can be defined as the ratio of the vertical distance between the zero and the fitted regression line to the vertical distance between the zero-correlation and perfect-correlation lines. An alternative and equivalent definition is that the correlation equals the ratio of the slope of the fitted line to the slope of the perfect-correlation line. Although the correlation coefficient is fundamentally based on the notion of the perfect-correlation line, such lines are virtually never drawn. However, for illustrative purposes we repeatedly draw such lines throughout this primer.

The correlation coefficient is commonly symbolized by r or ρ (rho, a Greek "r"), and a fact not well known is that this r comes from the first letter in regression. In actuality, the correlation coefficient estimates not the regression but rather the amount of nonregression. The relative distance from the perfect-correlation and the guesstimate lines (i.e., the amount of regression) equals $1 - r$. In this example, the observed regression line has regressed about 45% of the way from a perfect relationship.

The distance from the regression line to the perfect-correlation line gives the amount of regression toward the mean. Regression toward the mean measures how far from perfection the correlation is. Because the regression line can never be steeper than the perfect-correlation line, there is inevitably regression toward the mean. Again, we emphasize that the definition of regression toward the mean is

Regression toward the mean = Perfection – Correlation

So anything that makes correlations less than 1 creates regression toward the mean.

Note that the distance of the regression line from the perfect-correlation line is greater for more extreme scores. As can be seen by examining Figure 1.6, if the pretest or X is 4 or 24, the regression line is about 5 units from perfection and so the amount of regression expected is 5 units. If the pretest is 9 or 19, it is about 2.5 units from perfection. Finally, if the pretest is 14, the mean, it is right on the perfect-correlation line and there is no regression toward the mean. As the scores move from the mean, either up or down, the distance from perfection (i.e., regression toward the mean) increases. The more extreme the score, the greater the regression toward the mean.

We hope that the reader has gained some understanding of the relation of the correlation coefficient to the regression line (the line of best prediction of one variable from another). We hope that by visual estimation and graphical procedures, we have increased the comprehension than what is more typically achieved by the usual computation of a correlation coefficient. However, for a general understanding, this demonstration is limited by the fact that we introduced into the process prior knowledge to provide the approximate value of the pretest and posttest means, as well as knowledge that these means were equal and that the variability of pretest and posttest was equal. In Chapter 2, we generalize the method and such knowledge is not required.

THE PAIR-LINK AND GALTON SQUEEZE DIAGRAMS

In our pedagogy, we have repeatedly found that the scatter plot and the regression line do not illustrate regression toward the mean very clearly. Our students often make elementary errors even after repeated exposure to these diagrams. To better illustrate the phenomenon, we introduce a new type of illustration: the *pair-link* diagram. Although others (Wohlwill, 1973) have used similar diagrams, we believe that we are the first to feature it as an alternative to a scatter plot. It does, however, bear a close resemblance to a "spaghetti plot" in growth-curve analysis. (This is called a spaghetti plot because it looks like uncooked pasta tossed on a flat surface.)

Figure 1.7 shows in a pair-link diagram the same data that were presented in Table 1.1 and Figure 1.1. In a pair-link diagram, there are two vertical lines: the line on the left refers to the pretest; the line on the right, the posttest. Each person is plotted twice. The pretest score is plotted on the left vertical axis, and the posttest score is plotted on the right vertical axis. These two points are connected by a straight line and hence the name pair-link diagram. Every point in a scatter plot is a line in the pair-link diagram.

It is helpful to see the equivalence of the two types of dia-

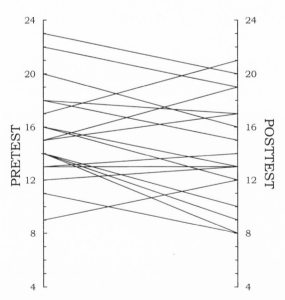

FIGURE 1.7. Pair-link diagram of the data in Table 1.1 and Figure 1.1.

grams. Locate the one person who has a pretest score of 20 and a posttest score of 16 in both Figures 1.1 and 1.7. As a second example, locate the person (actually two persons) with a 13 on both the pretest and the posttest. The reader should confirm in his or her own mind that these two diagrams present the same data but in very different ways.

Actually a pair-link diagram is rather similar to a space–time or Minkowski diagram in physics. We plot where the person is in a "variable space" at the pretest and where the same person is at the posttest. Then we connect those two points by a straight line that approximates the way in which the person "traveled" through time from pre- to posttest.

Figure 1.8 shows the pair-link diagram with the posttest scores averaged or squeezed for the 20 or so possible pretest scores for the data set with 500 "persons." The points on the left are the possible pretest scores, and the scores on the right are the posttest means for each of these pretest scores. We then draw a line from the pretest value to the average value on the posttest. To make clear which scores are squeezed or averaged, the arrow at the top of the diagram points toward the averaged or squeezed axis. We call Figure 1.8 a

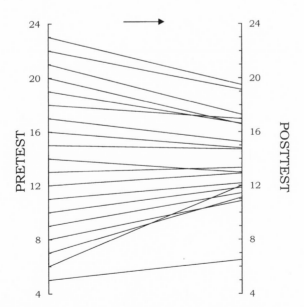

FIGURE 1.8. Galton squeeze diagram for the data set with 500 cases using pretest to predict posttest.

Galton squeeze diagram, which is based on the pair-link diagram for these data. The Galton squeeze diagram corresponds to the overfitted zigzag regression line of Figures 1.5 or 1.6, but it much more dramatically illustrates regression toward the mean. For each value on the pretest, for example, the pretest values of 8 and 20, the average posttest value is computed and graphed. When this is done for all pretest values, one has the full Galton squeeze diagram. The reader should compare this figure with the zigzag overfitted regression line of Figures 1.5 or 1.6 by looking at the lines that crossover. If there were a perfect picture in Figure 1.8 (i.e., no sampling error), none of the lines would cross each other. Note that the lines from pretests 6 and 7 do crossover,[5] and this corresponds to a departure from the regression line in Figure 1.6.

A Galton squeeze diagram dramatically illustrates the regression toward the mean in the data. The more extreme scores change more than the less extreme scores. With a Galton squeeze diagram, we can actually see the regression toward the mean more clearly than we can with a scatter plot.

It is instructive to consider what a Galton squeeze diagram would be for different values of the correlation coefficient. If the correlation were zero, all of the lines would theoretically converge to a single point, the posttest mean. Figure 1.9A illustrates the pattern for a zero correlation. All the lines do not converge at exactly the same point due to sampling error. The diagram clearly shows that there is complete regression toward the mean. If the correlation were perfect, then the plot would be a set of straight parallel lines that do not intersect, as in Figure 1.9B. We defer illustrating what the diagram would look like for a negative correlation until Chapter 2.

The first author has previously used idealized Galton squeeze diagrams to illustrate regression toward the mean (see Figures 1b and 1c in Campbell & Stanley, 1963). We name this diagram after Galton because this was the form in which he discovered regression toward the mean. In place of a pretest, he had a parent's height; in place of a posttest, he had the height of an adult child. He came to the biological conclusion that nature was causing the extremes to "revert" or "regress" toward the species mean, a conclusion that he later retracted when he noticed that regression toward the mean occurred backward in time, a topic that we now consider.

---

[5]We could smooth the Galton squeeze diagram by plotting not the means but rather the predicted "mean" from the regression line. There would be no crossovers in such a plot.

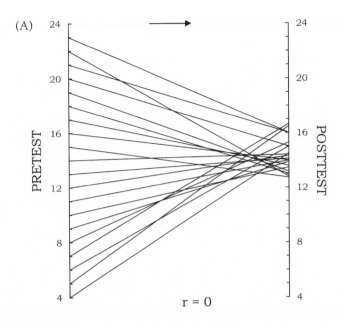

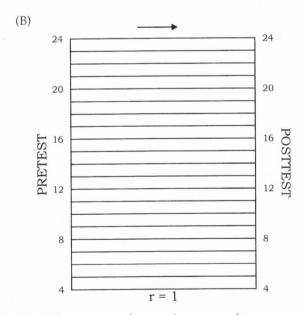

FIGURE 1.9. Galton squeeze diagram (pretest predicting posttest means) for (A) a zero correlation and (B) a perfect correlation ($N = 500$).

BACKWARD PREDICTION

It is necessary to examine not only how well the pretest predicts the posttest but also how well the posttest predicts the pretest. Figure 1.10 presents the overfitted regression line using the posttest to predict the pretest, again with the same data set with 500 "persons." It might help to reexamine the scatter plot in Figure 1.3. For those scoring a 7 at the posttest, we have drawn a box. The mean of the scores in the box is 10.54, which is for the 7's in Figure 1.10. Note that the line in Figure 1.10 is much steeper than the one in Figure 1.6. However, if the plot were rotated clockwise by 90 degrees, the line would be nearly exactly as steep as the one in Figure 1.6. We have also drawn in Figure 1.10 both the perfect-correlation line and the zero-correlation line. We see again that the regression line lies about halfway between the zero-correlation and perfect-correlation lines, and so the correlation is about .5.

It is very important to run the regression analysis in both directions in time. Few statistics texts point out that there are two, not one, regression lines. The correlation coefficient is the same predicting in either direction. However, if means or the line are

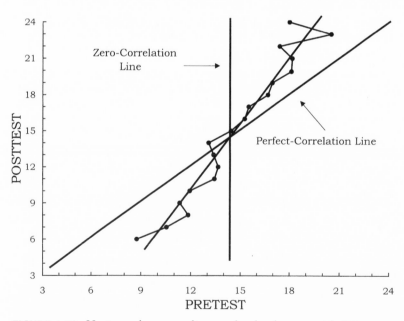

FIGURE 1.10. Horizontal squeeze diagram for the data set with 500 cases.

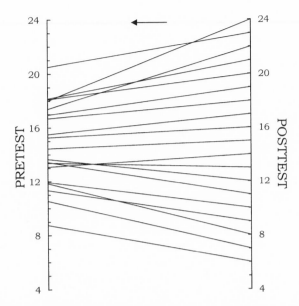

FIGURE 1.11. "Backward" Galton squeeze diagram for the data set with 500 cases (posttest predicting pretest).

"guesstimated," there will be some discrepancy between the two guesstimated correlations. The perfect-correlation line is the same regardless of the direction of prediction.

The Galton squeeze diagram can also be time reversed. Figure 1.11 shows the Galton squeeze diagram predicting from posttest back to pretest. The arrow points from posttest to pretest. Note that it is essentially, but not exactly, the mirror image of the pattern in Figure 1.8. Again, note the crossovers on the Galton squeeze diagram and match them with the larger departures from the linear regression line in Figure 1.9. The Galton squeeze diagram shows greater "change" backward in time for the more extreme scores. The large scores become smaller, and the smaller scores become larger.

BIOLOGY AND REGRESSION TOWARD THE MEAN

Galton initially viewed regression toward the mean as a biological fact. It is the case that biology needs to overcome regression toward the mean. Consider what would happen if children inherited the exact average of their parents' attributes. If that happened, then eventually, at least biologically, we would all be the same. But nature needs diversity for natural selection to operate, and so organisms each have two sets of chromosomes, one of which is passed onto their offspring. This form of inheritance prevents species from regressing toward the mean and so promotes biodiversity.

A GOLDEN OLDIE: McNEMAR'S ILLUSTRATION

Regression toward the mean is thus not a true process working through time but a methodological artifact, a tautological restatement of imperfect correlation (Campbell & Boruch, 1975). If one variable is used to predict another, the predicted score cannot on average be more extreme than the predictor. It is fitting that we close this chapter with one of the earliest illustrations in social science of this phenomenon, that of McNemar (1940), one of the original popularizers of this topic.

Suppose that the intelligence test scores of all the children in an orphanage are measured on two occasions, a year apart. Assume that the group mean and standard deviation are basically the same at both testings. If one examines the children with initially high scores, they will have regressed down toward the mean on a second test and will appear to have become worse. Those initially scoring lowest will have improved. One may mistakenly conclude that the orphanage is homogenizing the population, reducing the intelligence of the brightest and increasing the intelligence of the less bright. However, if one were to look at the extremes on the posttest and trace them back to the pretest, one would find that they were nearer the mean on the pretest, thus implying the opposite conclusion: variance appears to be increasing over time. These seemingly contradictory findings imply only that the test–retest correlation is less than perfect. When correlations are less than 1, there will be regression toward the mean.

CONCLUSION

The major focus of the chapter is a graphical introduction of regression toward the mean. We have used the scatter plot and two new graphical methods: the pair-link diagram and the Galton squeeze diagram. The pair-link diagram, which contains exactly the same information as the scatter plot, consists of two vertical lines, one for each variable. An observation is plotted on each line, and a straight line connects the two points. A Galton squeeze diagram is a pair-link diagram in which the possible scores of one variable are connected to the means on the other variable for that possible score.

The chapter also presents a graphical interpretation of the correlation coefficient. We introduced two lines that might be plotted. The first is the perfect-correlation line, which is what the regression line would look like if the correlation were 1. The second is the zero-correlation line, which is what the regression line would look like if the correlation were 0. The correlation coefficient can be defined as the ratio of the slope of the regression line to the slope of the perfect-correlation line. We hope that this has provided the reader with a better intuitive understanding of correlation.

When the regression line is plotted, the perfect-correlation line is hardly ever drawn and is difficult to visualize. The distance from the perfect-correlation line to the regression line is the amount of regression toward the mean. Thus, the perfect-correlation line should be drawn if we are to see the amount of regression toward the mean. Better than the regression line, the Galton squeeze diagram dramatically illustrates regression toward the mean. It vividly illustrates that regression toward the mean is greater the more extreme the score.

Finally, regression toward the mean occurs to the same extent whether we look backward or forward in time. This is a key fact that can be exploited in diagnosing regression artifacts in later chapters. Galton squeeze diagrams clearly show this forward and backward regression toward the mean. It is difficult to see the regression in both directions in a graph of the regression line, however, because it requires rotating the figure by 90 degrees. With a Galton squeeze diagram, the backward and forward diagrams are virtually mirror images of each other. If the reader were to learn nothing more than how to draw and interpret a Galton squeeze diagram, we would consider the primer to be a success.

Regression toward the mean is a fact. Because of a less than perfect correlation, the predicted score of a variable tends not to be as extreme in terms of standard score units than the predictor variable in standard score units. Over-time correlations are less than perfect because people change, and these changes imply that regression toward the mean is an omnipresent phenomenon. All too often the statistical fact of regression toward the mean is given a substantive meaning that is unwarranted.

One of the goals of this primer is to remove the mystery and mystique surrounding the concept of regression toward the mean. We must admit that at times the concept can be difficult. We shall see that sometimes the mistake is made to correct for regression toward the mean when none should be made. If the reader finds some of the concepts in this primer difficult, he or she should take comfort from the fact that some people who ought to have understood them had difficulties. Consider the following examples:

> Sir Francis Galton, generally considered one of the real geniuses of the 19th century (Simonton, 1994), was tricked by the phenomenon.
> Smith (1997) described how a Nobel laureate economist was fooled by the concept!
> One of us served as dissertation advisor on a project that was eventually shown to be a regression artifact (Reichardt, 1985).
> Mark (1986) describes how a prominent example in Cook and Campbell (1979) contains a regression artifact.

If the renowned Galton as well as a Nobel laureate, and even the authors of this primer have sometimes been fooled, the reader must be especially vigilant in detecting regression artifacts.

Next, in Chapter 2, we explore further the concept of regression toward the mean and provide a general definition of the concept. We develop the formal mathematics and answer frequently asked questions about the phenomenon. Finally, we generalize our graphical method to the case in which the means and variances are different for the variables. After that chapter, we begin our search for regression artifacts.

2

Mathematics and Special Cases

In the previous chapter, a graphical introduction of regression toward the mean was developed. We introduced the Galton squeeze diagram that clearly illustrates that more extreme scores "change" more than less extreme scores. In this chapter we examine regression toward the mean more generally and formally. Although we present formulas in this chapter, we still keep the discussion nontechnical and use graphical presentations whenever possible.

We also consider frequently asked questions about regression toward the mean. By answering these questions we hope to broaden and deepen the comprehension of the concept.

GENERALIZATION TO THE CASE WITH UNEQUAL MEANS AND VARIANCES

The graphical approach just presented in Chapter 1 rests heavily on the assumption that the two variables, pretest and posttest, have the same mean and variance. In this section, we allow for the more general case. We also do not presume that the mean is known as we did in the last chapter.

There are two variables, X and Y, which may have different means and variances. We focus on regression toward the mean in Y as a function of X. However, as was emphasized in the previous chapter, we can also look at regression the other way: X regresses toward the mean when Y is used to predict it. Regression toward the mean is inherently a bidirectional phenomenon.

We use an extension of the example from the previous chap-

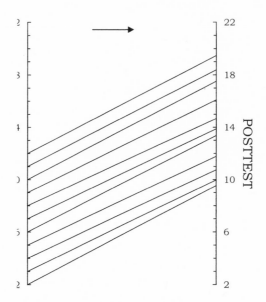

FIGURE 2.1. Galton squeeze diagram (pretest predicting posttest) for a case in which the means and standard deviations differ.

ter. There we took the sum of two dice as a "true score" and the sum of two more dice as "error." So the same true score was added to both pretest and posttest, but a different error score was added. Here, we treat the true score as X or the pretest, and the true score plus error is treated as Y or the posttest. We generated data for 500 "persons." The sample mean of X is 7.00, and its standard deviation is 2.45; the mean of Y is 14.06, and its standard deviation is 3.52. Quite clearly, the means and the standard deviations of the pretest and the posttest differ in that they are both increasing.

Figure 2.1 presents the Galton squeeze diagram for this data set. It appears that there is no regression toward the mean. All of the scores seem to be increasing by about 7 points. However, as will be seen, there is indeed still regression toward the mean.

Figure 2.2 contains the overfitted and regression lines using 500 scores with the true score or X used to predict the measured score or Y. Consistent with the Galton squeeze diagram in Figure 2.1, the regression slope[1] is near 1. (Parallel lines in a Galton

---

[1]If Y is used to predict X, we are using the observed score to predict the true score, something we called true-score correction. The regression slope for that prediction equation is .5, the reliability of the observed score.

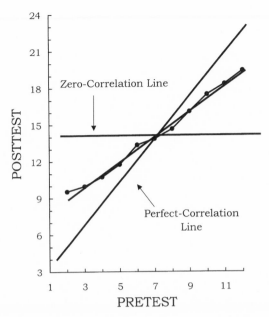

FIGURE 2.2. Overfitted, regression, zero-correlation, and perfect-correlation lines when the means and standard deviations differ.

squeeze imply a slope of 1.) It is difficult, if not impossible, to see regression toward the mean in Figure 2.2. In fact, because the slope is near 1, it appears that there is no regression toward the mean at all. However, if the variances differ, the slope of the perfect-correlation line is not a diagonal with a slope of 1, but rather it equals s_Y/s_X. It equals this value for the following reason. Note that if $Y = X$, then $s_Y = s_X$. However, if $Y = aX$, the standard deviations are unequal and, because $s_Y = as_X$, it follows that the perfect slope or a equals s_Y/s_X. So for a perfect correlation of 1.0, the slope equals the ratio of the standard deviation of the criterion to the standard deviation of the predictor.

For the example data set, this ratio of standard deviations equals 3.52/2.45, or 1.44. We have drawn the perfect-correlation line in Figure 2.2. Its slope is 1.44 and goes through the point $\{M_X, M_Y\}$. From the previous chapter, we learned that the correlation coefficient equals the observed slope divided by the perfect slope. For the example, we have 1/1.44, which equals .694. Given how the data were generated, the theoretical correlation is 1 divided by the square root of 2, or .707. The actual correlation is .724.

There is an alternative way to determine the perfect-correlation line that may be easier to understand. We rank order both X and Y from smallest to largest. We then plot X against Y; that is, we plot the largest score for X against the largest score for Y, the second largest, all the way to the smallest score. We draw a guesstimate line through this plot, and that is an estimate of the perfect-correlation line; the slope of that line approximately equals s_Y/s_X.

We can make the two variables always have the same mean and standard deviation by computing standard scores. A standardized or Z score takes each score and first subtracts the sample mean for that variable and then divides this difference by the standard deviation of the variable. The result of such a transformation is that the new variable, the standardized variable, always has a mean of 0 and a standard deviation of 1. So, if two variables are standardized, they necessarily both have the same mean and standard deviation.

Figure 2.3 presents the Galton squeeze diagram of the example data set with both variables standardized. We see that there is regression toward the mean, although the degree of regression is less than what it was in the previous chapter. There is less regression in this example because the correlation is much larger, .724 versus

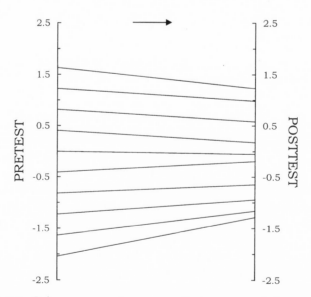

FIGURE 2.3. Galton squeeze (pretest predicting posttest) diagram using standard scores.

.503. Once the scores are standardized, extreme scores regress more toward the mean than do less extreme scores.

Let us consider two variables, X and Y, both of which are standardized. If we select an extreme score from X (i.e., a score distant from the mean of that variable), then the expectation in terms of Y is that the scores of that person or group of persons will not be as extreme (in terms of a standardized score). The degree of regression toward the mean is determined by how far the regression line is from the diagonal line. When scores are standardized, the slope of the regression line is identical to the correlation coefficient. So regression toward the mean occurs whenever the correlation is not perfect.

FORMAL DEFINITION AND FORMULAS

In this section, we present the formulas necessary for the exact computation of the amount of regression toward the mean. The formulas may provide some insight into the meaning of the concept.

We first consider the case in which both X and Y are standardized:

$$Z_X = \frac{Y - M_X}{s_X}$$

and

$$Z_Y = \frac{X - M_Y}{s_Y}$$

where M_X and M_Y are means and s_X and s_Y are standard deviations. Throughout, to simplify presentation, we drop the subscript i denoting a person. Predicted standardized Y or Z'_Y equals

$$Z'_Y = rZ_X$$

Regression toward the mean works in both directions, and so

$$Z'_X = rZ_Y$$

To forecast the amount of regression toward the mean when scores are standardized, we need simply to know the correlation between the scores.

So, for instance, if it is known that the correlation between husbands' and wives' marital satisfaction is .60 and it is known that a particular husband is very satisfied, say, 2 standard deviations above the husband mean, then we would expect his wife also to be satisfied, but not nearly as much. Her satisfaction would be .6 times 2, or 1.2 units above the wife mean. So the wife is very satisfied, though much less than her husband.

To express regression toward the mean in raw scores, we need to rearrange the above equation for Y' (the expected value of Y given X):

$$Y' = M_Y + r(s_Y/s_X)(X - M_X)$$

Because the regression coefficient in which X is used to predict Y, symbolized by b_{YX}, can be shown to equal $r(s_Y/s_X)$, we substitute b_{YX} for $r(s_Y/s_X)$:

$$Y' = M_Y + b_{YX}(X - M_X)$$

In a similar fashion, we can express the predicted X given Y:

$$X' = M_X + b_{XY}(Y - M_Y)$$

where b_{XY} can be shown to equal $r(s_X/s_Y)$. So, to forecast the regression toward the mean, we need to know the slope and the means of both variables.

For over-time data and for some other applications, it is sometimes assumed that the means and standard deviations of X and Y are the same. If this assumption can be made, the prediction equations are:

$$Y' = M + r(X - M)$$

and

$$X' = M + r(Y - M)$$

where M is the common mean for X and Y. For many of the illustrations in the subsequent chapters, we use these equations.

Note that the above equations can be reexpressed:

$$Y' = (1 - r)M + rX$$

and

$$X' = (1 - r)M + rY$$

The predicted score can be viewed as a weighted average of the predictor variable and the mean. Note that the weights sum to 1 $[(1 - r) + r = 1]$. The prediction equation states how much to weight what is known about a particular case (X or Y) based on what is known about the group (M). The equation states the degree to which the overfitted regression line lies between the perfect-correlation line and the zero-correlation or perfect-ignorance line (see Figure 1.6 in the previous chapter or Figure 2.2 above in this chapter).

One important application of this last set of formulas is called the *true-score estimate* (Cronbach, Gleser, Nanda, & Rajaratnam, 1972). Of course, the true score is not known, but if we can theoretically regress the true score on the observed score, the resulting regression coefficient is the variable's reliability. So the true-score estimation formula is

$$X'_T = r_X(X - M_X) + M_X$$

where X'_T is the predicted true score, r_X is the reliability of X, and M_X is the mean of X. What the correction does is predict what the true score would be given the measured score, accounting for the fact that the true score and measured score do not have a perfect correlation (i.e., there is regression toward the mean).

The reliability can be viewed as the correlation between the test with a parallel measure. A parallel measure is assumed to have the same mean and variance as the other measure. To use the true-score estimate, previous research must be done so that r_X and M_X are known.

To illustrate the use of this formula, if a person's score is 2 standard deviations above the mean and the reliability is .75, then the estimated true score in Z-score terms is $.75 \times 2.0$, or 1.5. Given a normal distribution, the score changes from the 98th percentile to the 93rd percentile. Note that the predicted true score is always less extreme than the raw score; that is, it regresses toward the mean.

The variance of predicted true scores is always less than the variance of raw scores. The technical name for the reduced variance is *shrinkage*. One reason why true-score estimation is not often done is that the correlation between X and X'_T is 1. Thus, for many analyses, the correction has no effect on the results. Nonetheless, as we shall see throughout this primer, true-score estimation can be informative. We believe that true-score estimation is the most important psychometric formula that is not well known outside of psychometrics.

TABLE 2.1. Regression Formulas for Predicted Y and X (Y′ and X′)

Standardized score

$$Z'_Y = rZ_X$$
$$Z'_X = rZ_Y$$

Raw score

$$Y' = M_Y + b_{YX}(X - M_X)$$
$$X' = M_X + b_{XY}(Y - M_Y)$$

Equal mean and variance

$$Y' = M + r(X - M)$$
$$X' = M + r(Y - M)$$

True-score estimate

$$X'_T = M_X + r_X(X - M_X)$$

Note. See the Glossary of Symbols for definitions of terms.

To summarize, there are four sets of regression prediction equations presented in Table 2.1. In the first, both variables are standardized and regression is a function of only the correlation between variables. In the second, and most general formulas, the raw scores are used. For these equations, the regression slope and the means of both variables are needed. In the third set of equations, the mean and variances of the two variables are assumed to be equal. To determine the degree of regression toward the mean, the correlation and the common mean are needed. Finally, if a variable's reliability is known, we can use the regression toward the mean formula to compute a true-score estimate from the raw score. We shall be using the equations in Table 2.1 to compute the degree of regression toward the mean in this and subsequent chapters.

FREQUENTLY ASKED QUESTIONS ABOUT REGRESSION TOWARD THE MEAN

In this section, commonly asked questions about regression toward the mean are answered. We suspect that many readers have these questions. By grasping the answers to these questions the reader may better understand the elusive concept of regression toward the mean.

Question 1: *Is it not the case that more extreme scores become even more extreme? Do not the rich get richer and the poor get poorer?*

For some variables as they change over time, extreme scores may become more extreme. However, the only way for this to happen is for the variance of the measure to also be increasing over time. Once the variances are equated by standardization, we obtain the usual regression toward the mean phenomenon. So if "the rich are getting richer and the poor poorer," the variance in income must be increasing over time.

A related point is that it is possible for all of the scores to be increasing over time (see, e.g., Figure 2.1), yet there is regression toward the mean. If all the scores are increasing, there must be an increase in the mean over time. Once an allowance is made for the increasing mean, scores above the mean at the pretest do not increase as much as scores below the mean. Regression toward the mean refers to standardized scores, not the raw scores.

Question 2: *If scores are regressing toward the mean over time, does that imply that the variance is declining over time and so there is increasing homogenization?*

The answer to this question is "No." Regression toward the mean refers not to the actual scores of a measure but to the predicted scores for that measure. For instance, if the correlation between pre- and posttest is 0, then the predicted score on the posttest is the mean of the posttest. This does not imply that all people have the same score, the mean. There are always errors in prediction, and these errors restore the variance. Besides, because regression toward the mean occurs in both directions, it is impossible for the variance to be both increasing and decreasing over time. Regression toward the mean does not imply increasing homogeneity over time.

Question 3: *How does the score "know" the mean, because the mean would be different if the sample were defined differently?*

So, for instance, if someone is just above the mean, that person should regress down toward the mean. But if a few of the smallest scores were dropped from the sample, that person would be below the mean and so now would regress up toward the mean. How can the same person both regress up and down toward the mean?

This is a difficult question, but it is indeed possible for the same score to regress both up and down, depending on how the sample is defined. In one case the score regresses down, and in the other the score regresses up. This seeming contradiction happens because regression toward the mean, although usually phrased in terms of an individual score, actually refers to the *sample* of scores. So, if the sample changes, the score can regress in a different direction. Also regression does not refer to raw change but to standardized change. Because standardization subtracts out the sample mean, the direction of regression might change if the sample mean changes.

Question 4: *Is measurement error the only source of regression toward the mean?*

Very often the claim is made that regression toward the mean is entirely due to unreliability. However, any factor that produces change (i.e., makes the correlation less than perfect), whether it is real change or measurement error, creates regression toward the mean. So even measures without any measurement error still show regression toward the mean, and it is a mistake to think that regression toward the mean is entirely due to unreliability of measurement. We return to this question in Chapters 5 and 8.

Question 5: *If the relationship is not linear, does that imply that regression toward the mean does not apply?*

When we fitted the line in Figure 1.5 in the previous chapter, we made the assumption that the line was straight. However, regression toward the mean does not depend on this assumption. Although linearity is an assumption in the computation of regression and correlation coefficients, linearity is not an assumption of regression toward the mean, at least in the most general sense of the term.

If the relationship between X and Y is nonlinear (i.e., not a straight line), it is possible for some scores actually to regress away from the mean. However, it must still be the case that the bulk of the scores regress toward the mean and the net result is regression toward the mean.

Consider the data in Table 2.2. The data take the form that $Y = X^2$ for values of X from 0 to 9, and the functional relationship between the scores is said to be curvilinear or quadratic. Table 2.2 also presents the standardized or Z scores for both variables. Let us consider the prediction of Y (i.e., X^2) using X. In Figure 2.4, we have graphed the relationship using standardized scores and have drawn the perfect-correlation line. When scores are standardized, the perfect-correlation line is always an ascending diagonal line (the 45-

TABLE 2.2. Nonlinearity Example (Y = X²)

X	Y	Z_X	Z_Y	X′	Y′
0	0	−1.43	−.97	1.57	−12
1	1	−1.11	−.94	1.67	−3
2	4	−.79	−.83	1.98	6
3	9	−.48	−.66	2.49	15
4	16	−.16	−.43	3.21	24
5	25	.16	−.12	4.14	33
6	36	.48	.26	5.27	42
7	49	.79	.70	6.61	51
8	64	1.11	1.21	8.16	60
9	81	1.43	1.79	9.91	69

degree line). We see that there is some regression away from the mean (or egression), in that some Y values above the mean are above the perfect-correlation line. Because the correlation between X and X^2 is .962, the perfect-correlation and regression lines are virtually identical. However, the bulk of the scores regress toward the mean in that they are below the perfect-correlation line when they are above the mean and above that line when below the mean. Overall, there is more regression than egression.

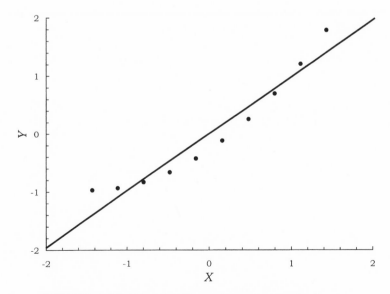

FIGURE 2.4. Nonlinearity illustration using standard scores.

Sometimes regression toward the mean is presented as requiring the assumption of linearity. It is our view that this requirement is unnecessary. If X is used to predict Y, the correlation is hardly ever 1 and a possible source of the imperfect correlation might be nonlinearity. As we have emphatically stated, the imperfect correlation and regression toward the mean are synonymous.

If the relationship between X and Y is nonlinear, then the researcher should attempt to model that nonlinearity. However, even if the researcher fails to model that nonlinearity, there is still regression toward the mean. It is true that some scores may egress from the mean, but the bulk of the scores still regress toward the mean.

Question 6: *Does a negative correlation imply that regression toward the mean does not hold?*

In this primer, we concentrate on the case in which the pretest is used to predict a posttest. Although there are some very rare exceptions (e.g., cycling processes; see Warner, 1998), almost always the correlation between these two variables is positive. However, correlations that are not test–retest correlations are sometimes negative. How do we interpret regression toward the mean when the correlation is negative?

We might be tempted to think that we have regression *past the mean*. That is, pretest scores above the mean tend to be below the mean at the posttest, and pretest scores below the mean tend to be above the mean at the posttest. In some sense, there is truth to this concept of regression past the mean. We again use dice rolls to generate 500 "persons," but this time we generate a theoretical −.5 correlation. The Galton squeeze diagram is contained in Figure 2.5 and does seem to indicate regression past the mean.

However, we believe that "regression beyond the mean" is not the most appropriate way to think about a negative correlation. For a negative correlation, a perfect correlation is not 1.00 but rather −1.00, a descending diagonal line. If X and Y have equal variance, then the slope of the line is −1 and goes through the point M_X and M_Y. If the variances are different, the slope is $-s_Y/s_X$ and again goes through the point M_X and M_Y. The estimated regression line falls between the flat horizontal line and the descending diagonal that is the perfect-correlation line for a negative correlation. So regression toward the mean is just as meaningful for negative as well as positive correlations.

Figure 2.6 uses the same data as in Figure 2.5, for which the correlation is about −.5. In Figure 2.6, we have drawn the overfitted

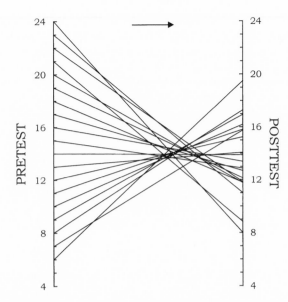

FIGURE 2.5. Galton squeeze diagram (pretest predicting posttest) for a negative correlation.

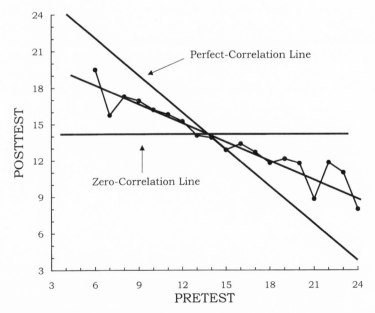

FIGURE 2.6. Overfitted, regression, zero-correlation, and perfect-correlation lines for a negative correlation.

regression line, the estimated regression line, the perfect-correlation line, and the zero-correlation line. The only difference between Figure 2.6 and the ones presented earlier is that the slope of the perfect-correlation line is negative. We see that the estimated regression line is almost exactly halfway between the zero-correlation line and the perfect negative correlation line, which is why the correlation is −.5. Note also that the farther from the mean the score is, the farther the score is from the perfect-correlation line. So negative correlations show the typical pattern of regression toward the mean. The key is that perfection implies the opposite score, not the same score.

Question 7: *How can there be regression toward the mean with a dichotomous variable?*

A dichotomous variable is a variable that takes on two values. For example, suppose that 100 persons take two tests and each test is graded pass or fail. If a dichotomy is scored "0" for fail and "1" for pass, the mean of the dichotomy represents the proportion of the sample that passed the exam. In Table 2.3, we have a set of counts from the two tests. There are four possibilities: pass–pass, pass–fail, fail–pass, and fail–fail (with the performance of the first examination listed first). Of the 100 students, 80 passed each exam.

Regression toward the mean is a difficult concept to understand with a dichotomy, because the mean is generally an impossible score for a person. The means in the example are both .8, but no one scores .8; a person can score only 0 or 1. However, the mean of .8 represents a probability. The regression line creates a prediction probability that is made for a particular score. Although that prediction may not be true of any particular score, it should be true of the average score.

Despite the scores being a dichotomy, there is still regression

TABLE 2.3. Numbers Passing and Failing Two Examinations

Exam 1	Exam 2		
	Pass	Fail	Total
Pass	70	10	80
Fail	10	10	20
Total	80	20	100

toward the mean. Someone who passes the first exam has an 88% chance of passing the second examination, whereas someone failing the first exam has only a 50% chance of passing the second exam. So, for both the person who passes and the person who fails the first exam, the expectation is that their performance on the second exam should be nearer to the mean than their performance on the first exam.

This case illustrates that the prediction involved in regression toward the mean refers not to a particular value but to a theoretical value. It is regression toward the mean, not regression toward the mode.

CONCLUSION

This chapter has taken the concepts introduced in Chapter 1 and generalized them. We have also provided the equations for regression toward the mean as well as answered some questions about the concept.

First, we have generalized regression toward the mean to the case in which the means and the standard deviations are not the same for the two variables. The perfect-correlation line is one whose slope is s_Y/s_X, where X predicts Y. The means and standard deviations can always be made equal by standardizing both variables (i.e., giving them both means of 0 and standard deviations of 1). The Galton squeeze diagram of standardized scores always exhibits regression toward the mean.

This chapter has presented the equations for computing the amount of regression toward the mean. These equations, which allow the researcher to calculate the exact degree of regression toward the mean, are used in subsequent chapters. We have also introduced the true-score estimation formula that states the estimated true score given an observed score.

Additionally, we have addressed commonly asked statistical and conceptual questions about regression toward the mean. We hope that our answers have helped clear up ambiguity that the reader might have about the concept. Regression toward the mean does not imply increasing homogenization as is sometimes mistakenly thought. We have elucidated topics that may occasionally confuse some readers: nonlinearity, negative correlations, and dichotomous variables. We show for each that regression toward the mean occurs.

We have also shown that the perfect-correlation line is different when the relationship is negative. In this case the perfect correlation line is a descending diagonal.

In the next seven chapters of this primer, we consider how regression toward the mean can bias the estimate of treatment effects as well as the measurement of change. As it progresses, this discussion increases in its complexity. We begin with the simplest designs and move on to more complex designs. We build on the concepts introduced in this and the previous chapter. We try to keep the discussion as nontechnical as we can, but we also wish to cover the material in as much depth as possible.

3

Regression Artifacts Due to Extreme Group Selection

Beginning with this chapter, we consider pseudoeffects that appear to be effects due to some supposed causal variable (e.g., an intervention) but are nothing more than regression toward the mean. We refer to such effects as *regression artifacts*. We see that these effects can be quite subtle yet their ultimate consequences may well be dramatic.

PRE–POST DESIGN AND REGRESSION ARTIFACTS

One preexperimental research design (Cook & Campbell, 1979; Campbell & Stanley, 1963; Judd & Kenny, 1981) is a study of changes for a group of treated persons. So, for instance, a group of children receive a new educational innovation and the researcher measures if their test scores improve. There is no control or untreated group, and the design is commonly called a *pre–post design*. Very often this design is used with a single person. For example, a person who suffers an illness all of sudden feels better after receiving a certain treatment.

We view this as a very uninformative research design. Campbell and Stanley (1963) labeled this design as *preexperimental*. However, we still consider it in detail because it is so prevalent and researchers, as well as consumers of research, all too often fail to consider regression toward the mean as an alternative explanation of change.

A simplifying assumption in this chapter is that if there were no intervention effects, the population mean of the group would not change over time. This is certainly a very strong assumption (for discussions of plausible rival hypotheses, see Campbell & Stanley, 1963; Cook & Campbell, 1979; or Judd & Kenny, 1981), but it is made to sharpen the focus on regression toward the mean.

Regression toward the mean is always a plausible rival hypothesis for mean change in the pre–post design. Only when the sample mean at the pretest exactly equals the population mean is there no regression toward the mean. Statistical theory implies that the probability of a sample mean exactly equaling the population mean is 0. So standard statistical theory predicts that regression toward the mean is inevitable. Just as change of individual scores is governed by the regression toward the mean phenomenon, so is change in means based on groups of individuals.

Even random selection of persons does not eliminate the plausible rival hypothesis of regression toward the mean. A random sample from the population does not guarantee that the sample mean *exactly* equals the population mean, just that *on average* the sample mean equals the population mean. The statistical significance test that the average change equals 0 can be reinterpreted: it demonstrates that the amount of change cannot be explained by regression toward the mean. What the significance test does is rule out the very plausible rival hypothesis that the change is due to regression toward the mean if it can be assumed that the sample is randomly chosen. For the pre–post design, random sampling is required for internal as well as external validity.

It is true that with random sampling, the sample mean should not be very extreme. The variance of the mean equals the variance of the observations divided by the sample size. So, given a reasonable sample size, it is unlikely that the sample mean would be very extreme, and extremity exacerbates the degree of regression toward the mean.

However, it is almost always the case that for the pre–post design individuals are nonrandomly selected. Nonrandom selection tends to create even more extreme groups, and so greater regression effects are to be expected. The researcher may often have some insight about the likely direction of the regression; that is, given regression, the scores are expected to go up (or down) over time. There are several factors that result in choosing extreme persons to be in the treatment group. First, many programs attempt to remediate a problem and so select persons who are most in need of intervention. Given regression toward the mean, we would expect these people "to improve." Other programs reward people for their past successes, and they select the scores of those who are doing the best. Given regression toward the mean, we would expect the scores "to decline." So a remediation program would appear to be beneficial, whereas a program that serves the more able would appear to be a failure because regression toward the mean was ignored.

How do we know whether there is selection of extreme scores? In principle, the scores of the entire population would be needed and, were they present, we could calculate the relevant parameters. We denote the pretest as X and the posttest as Y. Using formulas developed in Chapter 2 (see Table 2.1), the mean of the pretest and the posttest and regression coefficient relating pretest to posttest must be known. The formula for the predicted value of Y given X is

$$b_{YX}(X - M_X) + M_Y$$

If both X and Y are standardized (both have a mean of 0 and a variance of 1), the formula for the predicted posttest is much simpler:

$$rX$$

where r is the correlation between pretest and posttest and X is standardized. So if we have a score X and we want to predict Y, we need to know M_X, M_Y, and b_{YX}. So the amount of the regression depends on how extreme the scores are and how correlated the pretest and posttest are. So, for instance, if it can be assumed that persons are one-half a standard deviation above the population mean at the pretest and the correlation between pretest and posttest is .4, then the prediction is that the mean should be .2 of a standard deviation above the mean at the posttest.

The statistical literature provides more complicated schemes for correcting for regression toward the mean (Davis, 1976). However, these techniques too require knowledge of the distribution's parameters as well as an assumption that the shape of the distribution is normal.

The researcher virtually never has access to the population of scores and so cannot estimate the amount of regression toward the mean. If all of the scores are not available (as they hardly ever are), the researcher can only guess (though more somewhat sophisticated approaches are developed in this chapter as well as in Chapters 7 and 8). The essential problem with the pre–post design without random selection is that the exact amount of regression cannot be known. Only when there is a dramatic change in scores can the researcher be reasonably certain that the change cannot be plausibly explained by regression toward the mean. Weak effects are likely to be obscured by regression toward the mean. As is shown in this chapter, these regression artifacts can be substantial, in some cases as large as one-half a standard deviation.

We can estimate the population mean if we assume that it does not change over time ($M_X = M_Y = M$) and that all the change is due to regression toward the mean. The formula[1] for M is

$$\frac{M_Y - b_{YX}M_X}{1 - b_{YX}}$$

There is an interesting geometric interpretation of this formula: the population mean, or M, represents the point of intersection of the regression line (X predicting Y) and the perfect correlation line (X = Y). We use this formula for the rookie-of-the-year example later in this chapter.

We have assumed throughout the chapter that the extreme-score selection occurs only at the pretest or prior to it. Very often there is also selection of scores after the pretest and even at the time of posttest. This type of selection effect is usually referred to as *mortality* (Campbell & Stanley, 1963; Cook & Campbell, 1979). We do not consider this additional complication in this primer. We do note that we are in better position to study this type of selection because we do have pretest measurements on those who dropped out of the study.

EXAMPLES

If regression toward the mean is an inevitable feature of data, then it should translate into everyday observations. We recommend the discussions of Gilovich (1991) and Smith (1997) of regression toward the mean in everyday life; see also the classic discussion of the topic by Kahneman and Tversky (1973). Among other topics that

---

[1]In Chapters 5 and 8, we discuss the sources of selection. Here we are assuming that the source of selection is the score itself (a reasonable assumption for the rookie-of-the-year example later in this chapter). In some cases, it may be necessary to divide b_{YX} by the pretest reliability.

Gilovich considers is why parents think that punishment is more effective than rewards: because children are punished when they perform poorly, they are almost guaranteed to improve over time; and because rewards are given when children do well, they are almost guaranteed to do worse. In this section we consider several extended illustrations, many of which have not been previously discussed by Gilovich (1991) and others.

All in the Family

The prototypical example of regression toward the mean, discussed in Chapter 1, is parent's height predicting child's height. In this section, we present several new familial examples.

A common theme in novels is that children do not live up to the standards of their parents. A parent earns billions of dollars by developing a great company. He or she later gives the company to the children, and they do not achieve the great success of their parent. Quite clearly earning billions of dollars is an extreme event. So regression toward the mean predicts that the child will not be as successful as the parent. If we expect regression toward the mean for height, why should we be surprised to find it for intelligence, creativity, and hard work?

A related example is a hypothesis advanced about why there is so much current controversy about standardized testing. According to psychometrician Lloyd G. Humphreys (1986), the campaign against standardized testing is led by successful parents whose children do not perform very well on standardized tests. Because of regression toward the mean, it is all but inevitable that very intelligent parents will have less intelligent children. These parents want their children to have the same societal rewards as they did despite the fact that their children are much less intelligent than they are. Ironically, these parents are using their superior intelligence to argue that intelligence testing is invalid to aid their less intelligent children.

There is another family-related phenomenon that can be explained by regression toward the mean. The research evidence very convincingly shows that similar people are romantically attracted to one another (Epstein & Guttman, 1984). (The one major exception is gender: most men prefer women and vice versa.) Nonetheless, people persist in thinking that "opposites attract." Perhaps we fail to take into account the regression toward the mean effect and that is why people believe opposites attract when usually they do not. So, when we observe a very nasty husband who is married to a fairly pleasant woman, we mistakenly think that the nasty person should be paired with another very nasty person. However, even if the correlation is fairly positive, the statistical expectation is that the degree of nastiness should not be all that similar. Note that if the correlation is .5, the variance in the difference between two persons is equal to the variance in the scores. Overall, similarity still results in large dissimilarities between particular spouses, and the dissimilarity is expected to be greater when one of the scores is more extreme.

The Sophomore Jinx

One of the most important honors in major league baseball in North America is the rookie-of-the-year award. It is awarded to the best first-year player in each of the two major leagues. Through the years, it has been noticed that, more often than not, the winner of the rookie-of-the-year award does not perform as well during his second year. Such a phenomenon has been dubbed the *sophomore jinx* or *slump*.

Table 3.1 presents the rookie and sophomore batting averages from the 39 award winners from 1970 to 1994 who were hitters. For those not familiar with baseball, a batting average is the proportion of number of times that the batter has a hit (a good thing in baseball). An average of .300 is considered quite good, and below .200 is considered very poor. The data are also presented in a scatter plot in Figure 3.1, and a regression line is drawn. The data do indeed seem to indicate a sophomore jinx; using some of the same data, Taylor and Cuave (1994) obtained a similar result. In Table 3.1, note that 28 hitters declined and only 11 improved. The mean batting average for the rookie year is .285 and for the sophomore year is .266. For those who worry about statistical significance, a .019 decline is highly statistically significant [$t(38) = -3.49, p < .002$]. The effect size, using Cohen's d (Cohen, 1988) and the sophomore year as the base, is $-.56$, which is generally viewed as moderate in size. A .019 difference in batting average may seem trivial to some, but it can mean a million-dollar salary increase. Although on average rookies decline in their performance, there are exceptional rookies like Cal Ripkin, Jr., whose average increased 54 points in his sophomore year.

Baseball pundits have given several explanations of the sophomore jinx. One is that in the second year the pressure has been in-

TABLE 3.1. Batting Averages of Rookie-of-the-Year Award Winners for Their Rookie and Sophomore Years

Winner[a]	Rookie average	Sophomore average
TMA70	.302	.251
EWN71	.260	.258
CCA71	.275	.292
CFA72	.293	.246
GMN73	.300	.287
ABA73	.337	.233
BMN74	.309	.300
MHA74	.323	.303
FLA75	.331	.314
ADA77	.282	.253
EMA77	.283	.285
BHA78	.266	.314
LWA78	.285	.286
AGA79	.287	.254
JCA79	.285	.302
JCA80	.289	.210
SSA82	.282	.281
CRA82	.264	.318
DSA83	.257	.251
RKA83	.254	.215
ADN84	.284	.287
VCN85	.267	.232
OGN85	.273	.250
JCA86	.240	.257
BSA87	.300	.248
MMA87	.289	.260
CSA88	.271	.260
WWA88	.250	.233
JWN89	.293	.263
DJN90	.282	.275
SAN90	.290	.217
JBN91	.294	.273
CKN91	.281	.297
EKN92	.257	.247
PLN92	.290	.244
MPN93	.318	.319
TSN93	.283	.287
RMN94	.306	.285
BHN94	.282	.168

[a]The first two letters represent players initials, the third letter represents the major league (A, American; N, National), and the last two numbers represent the year.

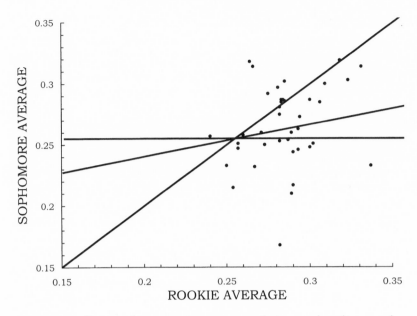

FIGURE 3.1. Scatter plot, regression, zero-correlation, and perfect-correlation lines of the rookie and sophomore years of 39 rookie-of-the-year winners in major league baseball from 1970 to 1994.

creased by winning the award and that creates performance anxiety. A second explanation is that the motivation to play well declines in the second year. This explanation is clearly explicated by the Denver Broncos' football running back Terrell Davis (*Denver Post*, Monday, September 9, 1996, p. 3D): "People who go for that [the sophomore jinx] do well their first year then stop listening to people. They start believing their newspaper clips. They did well and don't work hard."[2] However, the strongest and most plausible account of the jinx is regression toward the mean. Because of changes in motivation, ability, experience, and luck, there likely will be a decline in performance.

Can regression toward the mean account for the sophomore jinx? To be rookie of the year, the player needs to have an exceptional season: the player must be the best new player in the league. We would then expect that the player would not play quite as well

---

[2]It turns out that Davis's performance did not regress to the mean. He rushed for 421 more yards in his sophomore season than in his rookie season.

the next year. So the most likely explanation is regression toward the mean.

In Figure 3.1, we have drawn the perfect-correlation line. We have assumed a stationary model; that is, the mean and variance are the same during the rookie and sophomore years. We have drawn the zero-correlation line so that it intersects where the estimated slope also intersects the perfect-correlation line. We see that the zero-correlation line intersects the Y-axis at the .253 value, and we can treat this value as the mean of the population. Given this value of the mean, every rookie of the year but two (the smooth-fielding Julio Cruz and Walt Weiss) hit better than average, but 14 of the 39 hitters were below the extrapolated mean during their sophomore years.

The .253 average is about 10 points less than the major league average for this period of .263 (Thorn, Palmer, & Gershman, 1997). We can think of four different explanations for this discrepancy:

> There is in fact a sophomore slump.
> The distribution of major leaguers is truncated in that the very poor players are dropped from their teams. Thus, the distribution for rookies is more representative.
> There may be a maturation effect such that younger players (i.e., rookies) have lower batting averages.
> Because better hitters have more at bats than weaker hitters, the overall average is upwardly biased.

We think the sophomore slump explanation is not likely because it would predict a higher average for the third year and beyond, which appears not to occur (Taylor & Cuave, 1994). We believe that the last explanation is the most plausible of the four.

There are relatively few rookies each year, and so rookies' performance would not be that extreme. We would expect even more regression toward the mean if the analysis were done for each league's most valuable player, because many more players are eligible (Harrison & Bazerman, 1995). The more extreme the score, the greater the regression toward the mean.

Editorial Burnout

It might be thought that only statistically naive lay people fail to recognize regression toward the mean. The following illustration shows that statistical "experts" are just as subject to this lapse as are statistical novices. It is commonly observed that the careers of persons who become editors of major psychology journals go downhill after they have become editors. Usually it is said that the editor was burned out because of the heavy workload of editing a major journal. The second author of this primer has been repeatedly cautioned not to take on such an editorship position because it would destroy his career.

We do not know if the same sorts of claim are made for editors in other fields besides psychology, but we suspect that they are. Psychologists fail to take into account the regression toward the mean as an explanation. To be chosen as an editor requires that the person be a very successful researcher. The expectation, given regression toward the mean, is that currently very successful researchers should become less successful some 5–10 years later. Thus, the supposed "burnout" of editors is much more plausibly explained by regression toward the mean.

Harrison and Bazerman (1995) described the "winner's curse." Whenever someone is selected from a large pool (e.g., a job candidate is selected from a pool of hundreds of applicants), that person is very unlikely to live up to his or her billing. The larger the pool from which the editor or job candidate is selected, the greater the regression toward the mean—and because we all too often fail to adjust for regression toward the mean, the greater the disappointment.

Spontaneous Remission

Sapirstein (1995) reviewed 19 studies of the effect of psychotherapy and drug therapy on depression. In each study, researchers created a no-treatment control condition. For instance, several studies used a no-treatment, wait-list control group (i.e., those who were waiting to be in therapy). Sapirstein (1995) looked at the "improvement" of these untreated persons.

Table 3.2 presents the measures of change in each of the 19 studies. The measure that Sapirstein used is the change in depression divided by the pooled standard deviation at both times, a common measure of effect size called Cohen's d. Most of the studies used a standard measure of depression such as the Beck Depression Inventory.

Although there is considerable variability in the amount of change, the average is $-.35$ [$t(18) = -8.97$, $p < .001$]. According to

TABLE 3.2. Spontaneous Changes in Depression across 19 Studies

Study	Change	Study	Change
1	−.97	10	−.16
2	.28	11	−.48
3	.04	12	−.74
4	.12	13	−.11
5	−.21	14	−.41
6	−.42	15	−1.00
7	.03	16	−.27
8	−.34	17	−1.45
9	−.36	18	−.21
		19	.02

Note. Change measure in standard deviation units. So a score of −.50 means a decline in depression of one-half a standard deviation. Data from Sapirstein (1995).

Cohen (1988), .3 is considered a moderate effect size. So, people are becoming much less depressed even when they are not treated at all. These people improved on their own without benefit of professionally delivered intervention. Of course, some might have improved because they obtained nonprofessional psychotherapy from friends or family.

The Sapirstein (1995) review dramatically illustrates regression toward the mean. (The other explanations of change—history, maturation, and testing—do not seem like plausible explanations of the result.) Many people seek therapy when they are having a depressive episode. Not surprisingly, being *extremely* depressed leads people to seek out therapy. For many, though certainly not all, the depression wanes over time, even without the benefit of therapy. Although the improvement is a statistical necessity, people do in fact feel less depressed. The improvement is, at least in part, real. Although people may improve without therapy, they likely improve even more with it. So just because this analysis demonstrates regression toward the mean, it does not demonstrate that regression toward the mean entirely explains the effect of therapeutic interventions.

That people get better without any special intervention has been well noted by clinical researchers. It is commonly called *spontaneous remission*. Even though some investigators have noted that spontaneous remission can be explained by regression toward the mean, it is not generally recognized by theorists and practitioners.

Spontaneous changes have been noted in other areas of research. Consider two such illustrations:

Andrews and Harvey (1981) have noted that stutterers spontaneously improve without treatment ($d = -.19$).

Whitney and Von Korff (1992) have noted that those suffering pain experience substantially less pain a year later ($d = -.58$).

No doubt there are many other examples.

It seems likely that regression toward the mean leads people to believe in the efficacy of scientifically unjustified regimens. People who improve in health because of consuming snake oil and hearing the incantations of holy people no doubt would have improved without any such "therapeutic" interventions. However, the people who do improve attribute their better health to these unproven interventions and not to regression toward the mean. Many a quack has made a good living from regression toward the mean.

Misclassification of Individuals

Very often in life, people receive benefits or punishments based on their performance on tests. The previously discussed rookie-of-the-year award in baseball is one such example. But there are many other much more mundane examples. Assignment to special (i.e., remedial) or gifted education is often based on the performance on a test. Many medical procedures such as surgery are based on biological tests.

Generally, persons are selected for special programs when their scores are extreme. We have never heard of a school giving an award to a teacher or a student who is average. A common definition of an "extreme score" in applied settings is someone who scores 2 standard deviations above (or below) the mean on a test, a definition that we use. (A better definition would be 2 true-score standard deviations above the mean.) Given a normal distribution, there is about only a 2.5% chance of scoring that extreme.

These test scores, like any score, are subject to regression toward the mean. Moreover, because the scores are selected because of their extremity, there should be large amounts of regression toward the mean. Recall that the farther the score is from the mean, the greater the regression.

Consider the following hypothetical situation: a variable has a normal distribution and a test–retest correlation of .80 (the correlation between two administrations of the test). A .80 correlation may seem low, but it is a reasonable value for the test–retest correlation for many medical tests (e.g., two cholesterol tests taken on different days). It is probably fairly close to the test–retest correlation when there is a short delay and a different but parallel test is administered a second time.

Given that a person scores 2 or more standard deviations above the mean on one test, what is the probability that the person will score 2 or more standard deviations above the mean on a second test? Given the assumption of multivariate normality and a correlation between tests of .80, the probability is only .43. Thus, when someone is classified as "exceptional," most of the time he or she would no longer be so classified when retested. We suspect that even statistical experts would be surprised by how low this probability is.

There is surprisingly scant recognition of the misclassification problem in the applied literature. There are a few notable exceptions. Milich, Roberts, Loney, and Caputo (1980) showed in their study of those classified as hyperactive by use of a standard measure that only 45% were designated as hyperactive when a second test was used. Additionally, Anthony, LeResche, Niaz, Von Korff, and Folstein (1982) found that of those who were classified as suffering from dementia, 39% were misclassified. Flett, Vredenburg, and Krames (1995) found in their study that 40% of those who were initially classified as depressed on the Beck Depression Inventory were no longer depressed after retesting. Furlong and Feldman (1992) noted that regression toward the mean accounts for many misclassifications of children with learning disabilities.

We can ask the related but more relevant question: given that a person scores 2 or more standard deviations above the mean on one test, what is the probability that the person's true score is 2 standard deviations or more above the mean? The true score is the average of all possible scores that the person could receive. Again assuming multivariate normality and retest correlations of .80, that probability is .58. Given this result, a large percentage of people who are classified as gifted, learning disabled, or clinically at risk have been improperly classified given that being 2 standard deviations above or below the mean is the definition. Unreliability of measurement implies regression toward the mean, which in turn implies misclassification. Extreme scores do not likely remain extreme very long. The folk wisdom is correct: "When you are at the top, the only way is down."

Having two tests that are both extreme increases the probability of correct classification, but it does not totally eliminate the problem of misclassification. Consider three tests that all correlate with each other at .80. If a person scores 2 or more standard deviations above the mean on two tests, what is the probability that he or she will score 2 or more standard deviations above the mean on a third test? Given multivariate normality, this probability is .63. The probability that the true score is greater than 2 standard deviations above the mean if two tests are both greater than 2 standard deviations above the mean is .86. So, although having two extreme scores increases the probability of a correct classification, it does not guarantee it.

Psychometricians have long recognized that the expected score, given the observed score, is not as extreme as the observed score. As already discussed in Chapter 2, they have developed the true-score estimate (Cronbach et al., 1972). What the estimate does is predict what the score would be if regression toward the mean is accounted for. The formula is $r_X(X - M_X) + M_X$ where r_X is the reliability of measure X. To be able to compute true-score estimates, previous research must be done so that r_X and M_X are known. However, this is likely the case if the test is being used for classification purposes. So, for instance, if one's score is 2 standard deviations above the mean and the reliability is .75, then the estimated true score is .75 × 2.0, or 1.5. The person changes from the 98th percentile to the 93rd percentile. With shrinkage, it can be very difficult for a score to be extreme. Note that if r_X is 0, everyone is predicted to be at the 50th percentile. Unlike those folks at the mythical Lake Wobegan, where everyone is above average, here everyone is predicted to be average!

So, if one is classified "at risk" on the basis of a test, one should ask for the estimated true score, not the raw score, when the test result is presented. This corrected score provides a more realistic measure of the extremity of one's score.

Does regression toward the mean imply that we should not use tests to classify people? Certainly tests should be used, and when properly interpreted they provide essential information. However, we should realize that they are fallible. Extreme scores are never quite as extreme as they appear.

The more cynical among us might suspect that certain professionals have a vested interest in creating a large group of people who appear to be at risk though they are really not; so these professionals develop a criterion that overdefines the number "needing help" to provide employment for those in their profession. A more benign interpretation is that funding sources are unwilling to provide assistance unless someone is deemed to be severely at risk. Service providers assure the funding sources that only the very needy are being served (the bottom or top 2.5%), whereas in actuality the group is not as extreme as it might appear.

We return to the question of regression toward the mean and its role in prediction in Chapter 10. We see again that shrinkage is an important tool in making accurate predictions.

CONCLUSION

If a subsample of a population is selected, it may appear that the group is changing over time; however, that change may not be due to an intervention but rather to regression toward the mean. Even if the sample is randomly selected from the population, there is still regression toward the mean. Random samples have the desirable feature of their means being relatively near the population mean and so there is less regression toward the mean—but there still is some regression.

It may happen that regression toward the mean may obscure the benefits of a successful program. That is, if a group of individuals are above the mean and they are benefiting from the program, they might appear not to be changing at all. Conversely, the harmful effects of an intervention may be missed if the change due to regression toward the mean counteracts it.

Regression toward the mean is only one of several plausible rival hypotheses of change over time. *History, maturation, instrumentation,* and *testing* (see the Glossary of Terms for definitions of these rival hypotheses) are potentially plausible explanations of "change." However, regression toward the mean is perhaps the most pernicious plausible rival hypothesis because it is universal. The attribution of change in interventions is a very perilous process when the pre–post design is used. Randomized experiments have much to recommend them because they eliminate regression toward the mean as a plausible rival hypothesis.

In sum, causal inferences from the pre–post design are problematic. Even if we know that history, testing, and maturation hypotheses are implausible, in the absence of random selection regression toward the mean is a plausible explanation of the intervention effect. Only when the population parameters of the distribution are known can statistical corrections for regression toward the mean be made.

In the next two chapters, the design that we consider has a control group. We see that even with a control group, regression toward the mean still creates major interpretive problems.

4

Regression Artifacts
Due to Matching

We saw in the last chapter that it is problematic to examine how a group of persons changes over time and then attribute that change to an intervention. The actual cause of that change may be regression toward the mean. So, regression toward the mean is a plausible rival hypothesis in the pre–post design. In this chapter, we consider a second design that also has regression toward the mean as a plausible rival hypothesis: the nonequivalent control group design[1] with matching. In this type of study, there is a control group, which consists of untreated persons, and the pretest is used to "equate" groups by matching on that variable.

In this chapter and the next, we usually assume that persons are not randomly assigned to groups. So, if we were to compare the treatment and control groups on the outcome and were to obtain a difference in the means between the two groups, we would not know whether that difference was due to the intervention or whether it was due to the nonrandom assignment of persons to groups, what Campbell and Stanley (1963) called *selection*. Because of this plausible rival hypothesis of selection, the researcher attempts to adjust for selection using a second variable called a *covariate*. Two related strategies are used to adjust for the difference between groups on the covariate: matching and statistical equating. This chapter discusses matching, and Chapter 5 discusses statistical equating.

---

[1]We prefer the older and somewhat misleading name for this design of *nonequivalent control group design* to the more modern name of *nonequivalent groups design* (Cook & Campbell, 1979).

In matching, persons in the treatment and control groups who have the same score on the covariate or matching variable are included in the analysis. Those who do not have the same score (persons for whom there is not a match) are discarded from the analysis. In this way, the researcher artificially creates "equivalent" groups. In this chapter, we assume that the matching is on a pretest, but in many cases the matching is on some other variable which is categorical (e.g., ethnicity). Also sometimes a multivariate match is obtained; for example, persons are matched on age, ethnicity, gender, and motivation.

When matching is usually discussed, it is presented in terms of matching one individual in the treatment group with another individual in the control group; that is, there is a one-to-one matching. A much more practical approach is to identify all of those persons who have the same score on the matching variable in the treatment and control groups. In this case, there is a many-to-many matching.

Matching can be done prospectively or retrospectively; that is, the match can be obtained before the intervention is delivered (prospectively) or afterward (retrospectively). Most typically, matching is done retrospectively. However it is conducted, matching almost always results in some loss of data. Matches for some treated and control participants cannot be found. Usually it is advisable to have many more control units than treated units in order to match successfully all of the treated units.

The logic of matching is straightforward. Persons are not randomly assigned to groups, and so the groups are not equivalent. The researcher makes the groups exactly equivalent on the matching variable so that the groups are more comparable on the outcome measure. The danger of matching is that although the scores are more equivalent due to matching, it is unlikely that they are exactly equivalent. Thus, matching achieves more the illusion of equivalence than the reality.

Although we do not recommend matching of individual scores, we do recommend something that might be referred to as *group matching*. In selecting a control group, the researcher should try to find a group of persons who are demographically and experientially as similar to the treatment group as possible. So, if persons in the treatment group are children who attend a suburban high school, then the control children should also be from a suburban school. We would not use children who attend an urban school as controls.

Matching with random assignment results in unbiased estimates of treatment effects. In this situation, persons are first matched (prospective matching) and then randomly assigned to treatment conditions. Although some early simulation studies seemed to show that matching (called *blocking* in an experimental context) is superior to statistical equating (discussed in Chapter 5), work by Maxwell, Delaney, and Dill (1984) has clarified the comparison. When the assumptions of statistical equating hold, it is a more powerful statistical technique than matching.

In the analysis of matched data it is necessary to include the matching variable as a variable in the statistical analysis. Failure to do so would result in a loss of power (Chen, 1967), and so matching when improperly done may lead to too many Type II errors.[2]

DETAILED ILLUSTRATION OF THE LIMITS OF MATCHING

We present here a considerable update of Campbell and Boruch's (1975, pp. 213–222) and Campbell and Erlebacher's (1970) presentation of regression artifacts due to matching. The reader may wish to compare the discussion in this chapter with those articles. Also Furby (1973) presented an extended and clear discussion concerning the limits of matching.

Figure 4.1 sets up the hypothetical case of two elementary schools with student populations that differ in ability where the treatment is being given to the less able student population and the other group is used as the control. Presented in Figure 4.1 are the histograms for the two groups at (A) the pretest and (B) the posttest. The treatment group's histogram is denoted by the darker boxes, and the control group's by the lightly shaded boxes. As shown in the figure, the mean difference between the two groups and the variance within each group remain essentially the same on the pretest as on the posttest. In simulating this example, we used the rolls of four dice, a method described in Chapter 1 and Appendix A. We used the sum of four dice to create 500 treatment participants, and the sum of four dice with a 4 added for the 500 controls. Posttest scores contained two of the dice from the pretest rolls and two new dice. The sample sizes are much larger than in most quasi-experiments, but we want to reduce the role of sampling error in the presentation.

---

[2]We assume that matched units are more similar to one another than are units that are unmatched. Very rarely it happens that matched units are more dissimilar, and in this situation some of our conclusions would need to be reversed.

(A)

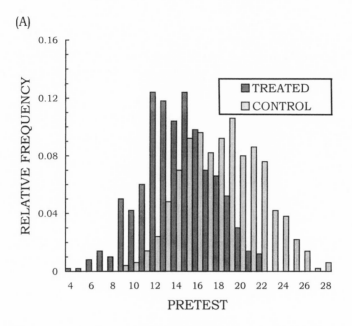

(B)

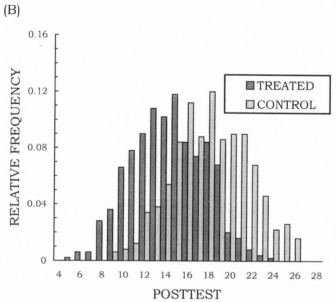

FIGURE 4.1. Histograms of the treatment group and control group at (A) the pretest and (B) the posttest.

Given the parameters of the simulation, the theoretical mean of the lower or treated group was set to 14 at both times and to 18 for the control group. We built into the simulation that the treated group scored less than the control group. The theoretical standard deviation is 3.42 for both groups and times. The theoretical size of the gap between groups is 4 units at both times; in terms of standard deviation units, the difference is 4/3.42, or 1.17. given that Cohen (1988) defined .8 as a large effect size, this is then a very large difference. We created a somewhat unrepresentative example to illustrate our points more sharply. A .5 correlation and regression coefficient was built into both samples. The statistics from the sample data differ slightly from these theoretical values and are presented in Table 4.1. That table shows again that the difference between the groups at both the pretest and the posttest is about 4 points. The same data set is used again in Chapter 5. (These two data sets can be obtained following the instructions in Appendix A.)

Figure 4.2 presents the data from the treatment group in a scatter plot. The parallel diagram for the control group is in Figure 4.3. Recall that an asterisk symbolizes 10 or more data points. For the moment, ignore the box in each diagram. Both diagrams show a positive correlation.

Given only this evidence, one conclusion would be that the hypothetical treatment given to the treatment group has absolutely no effect whatsoever. There is about a 4-point difference at both time points. The status of the two groups, both relative and absolute, is the same on posttest and pretest. Although this conclusion involves assumptions that we elaborate in the next chapter, it is the correct conclusion, in that it was built into the simulation.

TABLE 4.1. Basic Statistics for the Example

	Group	
	Control	Treatment
Pretest		
Mean	18.21	14.20
SD	3.66	3.32
Posttest		
Mean	18.10	14.29
SD	3.54	3.41
Correlation	.55	.49

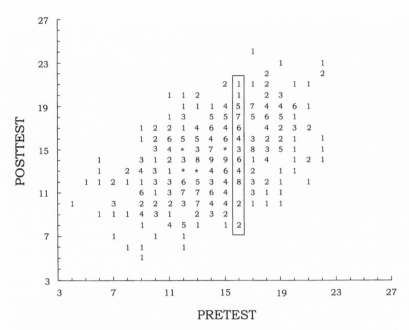

FIGURE 4.2. Scatter plot of pre- and posttest for the treatment group (asterisks indicate 10 or more observations).

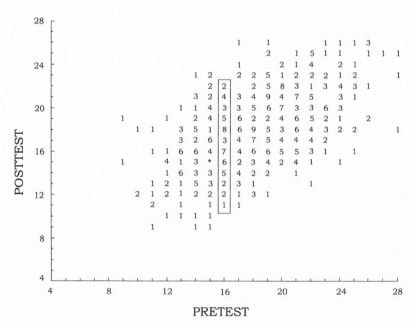

FIGURE 4.3. Scatter plot of pre- and posttest for the control group (asterisk indicates 10 or more observations).

In contrast to this conclusion, several seemingly more sophisticated approaches, matching and statistical equating, produce statistically significant effects—actually pseudoeffects! Although the true effect is 0, both matching and statistical equating yield effect estimates of about −2.0. We attempt to illustrate this result in intuitive detail in the case of matching in this chapter and statistical equating in Chapter 5.

Let us consider a rationale for matching: one should be bothered by the conspicuous pretest dissimilarity between the treatment and control groups of 4 points and feel that this dissimilarity made them essentially not comparable. It might be noted that despite this overall noncomparability, the two groups did overlap and must therefore contain comparable cases. This would suggest basing the quasi-experimental comparison not on the whole data set but only on subsets of cases matched on the pretest. Because there is overlap in the distribution, we can match scores that are the same at both times. So we are adopting a many-to-many matching strategy. Consider the scores that are 16, as they are on the boundary between the two distributions. There are 48 such scores in the control group and 49 scores in the treatment group.

Figure 4.4, a partial pair-link diagram, shows what happens to the two sets of 16's: Figure 4.4A presents the data from the treated units; Figure 4.4B, the data from the controls. Each of the two purified, compact, and matched subgroups on the pretest spreads out widely on the posttest, although each remains within the boundaries of its own group distribution. Because the subgroups on the posttest are no longer as pure, extreme, and compact as they were on the pretest, their means are being pulled toward the mean of their respective whole-group distributions. The posttest means are denoted by the wider lines. The control group scores are regressing up to 16.90, and the treatment group scores are regressing down to 15.12. The result is a separation of nearly 2 points in posttest means for the matched groups, which has often been mistaken for a treatment effect. Using the terminology of Campbell and Stanley (1963), we conclude that the plausible rival hypothesis of a matching study is selection by regression.

We can see the gap between the matched scores when we examine the overfitted regression lines in Figure 4.5. Recall from Chapter 1 that the overfitted line is obtained by averaging scores on the posttest for each possible score on the pretest. We have computed these overfitted lines for both the treatment and the control groups. Consider a particular pretest score, say, 16, and note that the controls outscore the treated units on that measure at the

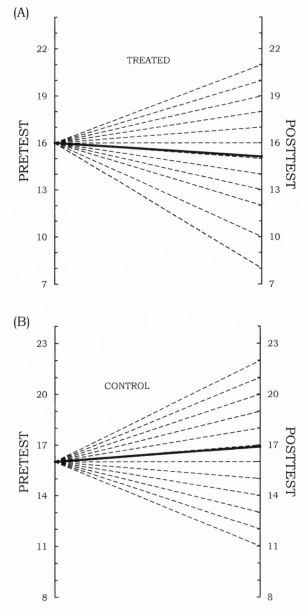

FIGURE 4.4. Pair-link diagram for those scoring 16 at the pretest: (A) treated units and (B) controls; bold solid line, the mean of all scores.

posttest: 15.12 for the treated group and 16.90 for the control group. Matching indicates a "treatment effect" of 15.12 – 16.90, or –1.78.

Not everyone in the sample can be matched. For the example data set, there is considerable overlap in the distributions and most of the scores can be matched. However, those scoring 23 and above in the control group and 8 or below in the treatment group cannot be matched. A total of 62 controls and 18 treated units cannot be matched.

With matching we get numerous measures of the "treatment effect," one for each set of matched pretest values. Each of these is indicated by the vertical distances between the two lines in Figure 4.5. Table 4.2 presents the different estimates of the treatment effect for each pretest score for which there are both experiential and control scores. The reader should try to find the estimates in Table 4.2 that correspond to the vertical distances in Figure 4.5. We see that the estimates range from .44 to –5.80, with the median estimate being –1.75. To get an overall estimate of the intervention effect across all values of the matching variable, these individual effects are averaged

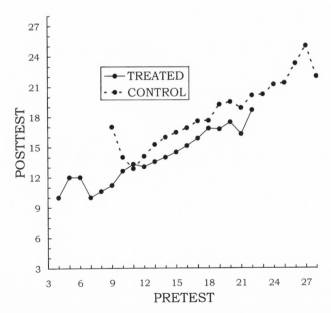

FIGURE 4.5. Overfitted regression lines using the pretest to predict the posttest.

TABLE 4.2. Posttest Means for Each Score on the Pretest

Score	Treated Posttest mean	n	Control Posttest mean	n	Estimate
4	10.00	1		0	
5	12.00	1		0	
6	12.00	4		0	
7	10.00	7		0	
8	10.60	5		0	
9	11.20	25	17.00	2	−5.80
10	12.62	21	14.00	3	−1.38
11	13.30	30	12.86	7	.44
12	13.05	62	14.08	12	−1.04
13	13.54	59	15.25	24	−1.71
14	13.98	52	15.97	35	−1.99
15	14.50	62	16.46	46	−1.96
16	15.12	49	16.90	48	−1.77
17	15.86	35	17.59	41	−1.73
18	16.85	33	17.63	46	−.78
19	16.77	26	19.23	53	−2.46
20	17.47	15	19.48	40	−2.01
21	16.29	7	18.88	43	−2.60
22	18.67	6	20.13	38	−1.46
23		0	20.24	21	
24		0	21.21	19	
25		0	21.36	11	
26		0	23.29	7	
27		0	25.00	1	
28		0	22.00	3	

in a statistically optimal fashion using analysis of variance. Because with matching we get many estimates of the treatment effect, we could allow for a treatment by matching variable interaction. It looks in Figure 4.5 as if the gap between the lines is less when the pretest is smaller. This effect is only apparent and not real. When we test for the treatment by matching variable interaction, the effect is not statistically significant [$F(13,892) = .84$].

Using the analysis of variance and treating the matched scores as a blocking variable, the estimate of the treatment effect is −1.73 and is highly statistically significant [$t(905) = 7.90, p < .001$; interaction set to 0]. Given how the simulation was created, the matching estimated "treatment effect" should be −2.00. Due to sampling error, there is some underestimation. Regardless, using matching results in the mistaken conclusion that the treatment is harmful.

Figure 4.6 presents the time-reversed overfitted regression lines for the treatment and control groups. In the figure, the posttest is used to predict the pretest. If Figure 4.6 were rotated clockwise 90 degrees, the pattern shown would be virtually identical to that in Figure 4.5. If we treat the pretest as the posttest and the posttest as the pretest, the "treatment" appears to look harmful. By reversing the flow of time we reach the same mistaken conclusion. In Chapter 10, we exploit the fact that time reversal can be used to detect regression artifacts.

The Galton squeeze diagram, introduced in Chapter 1, makes the bias in matching even more apparent. Recall that a Galton squeeze diagram is based on a pair-link diagram. Each point in a scatter plot becomes a line connecting the two vertical lines, the pretest and the posttest. In the Galton squeeze diagram, the lines are averaged on the posttest for each pretest value. Figure 4.7 presents a combined Galton squeeze diagram for the two groups. We have graphed only those scores for which there are at least 15 persons in both groups. The control group data are shown by dotted lines and the treatment group by the solid lines. It shows the diffi-

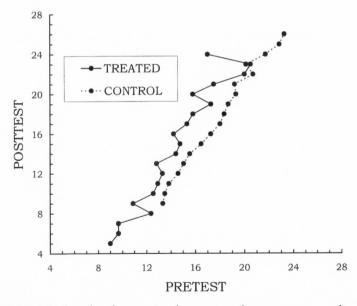

FIGURE 4.6. Overfitted regression lines using the posttest to predict the pretest.

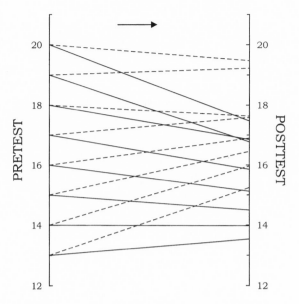

FIGURE 4.7. Galton squeeze diagram (pretest predicting posttest): solid lines, the treated group; dotted lines, the control group.

culty with matching. If the reader measures the divergence of matched pretest scores on the posttest, the difference tends to be about 2 points. Look carefully at the left side of Figure 4.7. The control group (the dotted lines) almost always outscores the treatment group.

Thus, the Galton squeeze diagram gives the same answer as the analysis of the scatter plot. The two groups are regressing to different means. So the matched control group scores are improving and the matched treatment group scores are declining. As was also shown in the scatter plot, the average difference between "equivalent" pretest scores on the posttest is about 2 points.

Figure 4.8 presents the Galton squeeze diagram using the posttest to predict the pretest. In essence, we are treating the pretest as the posttest and the pretest as the posttest. As in Figure 4.7, the control means are indicated by dotted lines and the treated group means by solid lines. To reduce the noise in the figure, we have included only those posttest scores where there are at least 15 persons in each group. This backward Galton squeeze diagram is the mirror image of the diagram in Figure 4.7. Looking from right to left, the matched control group scores are "improving" and the

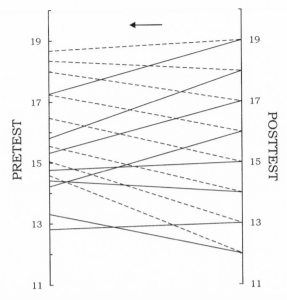

FIGURE 4.8. Time-reversed Galton squeeze diagram (posttest predicting pretest): solid lines, the treated group; dotted lines, the control group.

matched treatment group scores are "declining." It would seem difficult to argue that matching truly makes the groups equivalent.

DIRECTION OF BIAS

It is possible to forecast the likely degree of bias due to matching. This topic is discussed much more extensively in the next chapter, but in this section we anticipate some of those findings.

We begin with the data that were discarded in the matching process—those for whom there were not successful matches. (If all persons are matched in one of the groups, then we simply use the data from all persons, both matched and unmatched, to compute the means described below.) We locate those treated units and those control units for whom there were not successful matches. We scale the matching variable, the pretest for the example, so that its correlation with the outcome variable is positive. Next we compute the mean difference between the treatment and control groups of the unmatched scores on the matching variable. If this difference is positive, meaning that the treated group outscores the control group, then the likely case is that the treatment effect is overestimated. However, if the mean difference is negative, meaning that the control group scores higher than the treated group on the matching variable, then the likely direction of bias is that the treatment effect is underestimated. So, for the example, the pretest mean of the unmatched controls is 21.24 and the pretest mean of the unmatched treated units is 10.72. Thus, the likely (and in fact correct) direction of bias is negative. Matching results in an underestimate of the treatment effect. Because the treatment effect is 0, underestimation mistakenly makes the treatment look harmful.

Although the procedure that we suggest usually yields the correct conclusion, it is nonetheless possible to construct cases in which it is not. The limitations of this simple rule are discussed in the next chapter. Despite these limitations, we still feel that what we suggest is generally correct. In nonrandomized research, however, there is no absolute guarantee, even when sample sizes are large.

So the key data from a matching study are the scores of those who are not matched. What usually gets thrown away and ignored is critical information in a matching study. In every matching study of which we know, there is no report concerning this essential information. If matching is done (something we are very suspicious of), we strongly recommend that this information be presented and featured in the discussion of the results. As we discuss in Chapter 10, researchers need to know what is the likely direction of bias of the statistical methods that they employ.

CONCLUSION

Matching on a variable necessarily but artificially makes the groups equivalent. That equivalence is more of an illusion than a reality. Although matching can partially equate for the bias due to selection, it is typically only partially successful.

The likely direction of bias given matching can be determined by an analysis of scores that were not matched. If matching is used, the investigator should calculate and report this likely direction of bias, something that is hardly ever done.

It should be noted that the direction of bias is exactly opposite for the pre–post design and the nonequivalent control group design with a control group. In the pre–post design, ignoring regression toward the mean leads to pseudo-treatment effects for compensatory programs and underestimates for anticompensatory programs. Just the very opposite occurs with matching, and as we extensively show this same "effect" with statistical equating in the next chapter. The problem in the pre–post design is that regression toward the mean usually is ignored, which results in bias. However, in the nonequivalent control group design, the degree of regression toward the mean is overestimated when matching is used.

In the next chapter, we consider statistical equating, which is, in essence, only a more complicated version of matching. One problem with matching is that many cases might have to be discarded. With statistical equating, all of the cases can be used. However, regression artifacts plague statistical equating as much as they plague matching. From the perspective of this primer, both of these techniques make the same mistaken assumption.

5

Regression Artifacts Due to Statistical "Equating"

Matching requires that members of the treatment and the control groups score exactly the same on the matching variable. Statistical equating is like matching, but scores that cannot be matched can still be used. For instance, if someone in the treatment group scores 20 on the matching variable, there may be no controls who score 20. In addition, exact matching is difficult, if not impossible, when the treatment variable has many levels (e.g., the number of hours of treatment), though caliper or approximate matching is possible.

Statistical equating has the advantage that it uses all of the data and multilevel treatments do not present analytic difficulties. By using linear approximation, a prediction can be made concerning what the treatment and the control participants would score on the posttest. In matching, a degree of freedom is lost for each value of the pretest on which matching is done. Because statistical equating assumes linearity, it can be more efficient than matching (Maxwell et al., 1984). Despite these advantages of statistical equating over matching, the logic of the two methods is essentially the same. In essence, matching uses the overfitted line to make predictions, whereas statistical equating uses the regression line.

Statistical adjustment can (but probably never should) be used when the distributions of the two groups do not overlap. So, for instance, one might use preschool children as "controls" for an evaluation of a program for high school children. For such data, matching is impossible but statistical adjustment can be accomplished. This case is a linear extrapolation, whereas in the case in which there is overlap is a linear interpolation. Obviously linear extrapolation is a most perilous endeavor.[1]

Statistical equating has become so common that many researchers do not even realize that they are using the method. This chapter makes explicit the limits of the procedure. We hope that the reader will view analyses of quasi-experimental evaluations that use equating very differently after reading this chapter.

The variables used to equate groups are commonly called *covariates*. It is usually assumed that the relationship between the outcome and each covariate is linear, or a straight line. The linearity assumption should be tested; if nonlinearity is found, more complex relationships between the covariate and outcome should be estimated. To simplify the presentation in this chapter, the covariate is a pretreatment measure of the outcome and its relationship with the outcome is linear. Moreover, we assume that the slope of the relationship between the covariate and the outcome is the same in both groups (i.e., the covariate does not interact with the treatment variable).

We do not review the statistical details for making statistical adjustments, as they are presented in most statistics textbooks. Currently, the most common way to conduct such an analysis is through multiple regression. The covariates and the treatment variable are entered as variables in a regression analysis. An older alternative analysis is an *analysis of covariance*, or ANCOVA, and sometimes researchers compute partial correlation and residualized change score analysis (see Chapter 6). These methods are essentially identical to multiple regression. The advantages of multiple regression are that it is the most general method, it provides a direct estimate of the intervention effect, and there is no need to make complicated adjustments for the loss of degrees of freedom.

Sometimes covariates are included in the analysis to increase power. However, the primary use of covariates in nonrandomized research is to improve the internal validity of conclusions, that is, to rule out the plausible rival hypothesis of selection. Very often the inclusion of covariates in the analysis of nonrandomized designs actually lowers statistical power, especially when there is little overlap in the distributions.

As previously mentioned, we generally assume in this chapter

---

[1]As we discuss later in the chapter, the distributions do not overlap in the regression discontinuity design, yet this design has internal validity.

that the covariate is a pretreatment measure of the outcome. Thus, the covariate can be called a *pretest* and the outcome a *posttest*. A pretest–posttest design with a control group is called the *nonequivalent control group design* and is the most common quasi-experimental design. Moreover, statistical equating is probably the most common form of statistical analysis for this design.

LOOK AT THE "TREATMENT EFFECT" ON THE COVARIATE

It is important, but all too rarely done, to measure the difference between treatment groups on the covariate. This seemingly nonsensical analysis essentially treats the covariate as if it were the outcome by seeing if there is a "treatment effect" before the intervention is administered. It is absolutely essential to know the direction of the difference between groups on the covariate to be able to predict the direction of bias in the analysis of the outcome.

Sometimes there is more than one covariate. In such cases a *mega-covariate* is computed from the regression equation for the outcome. Within that equation, there are a sum of terms that are used to predict the outcome (e.g., $b_1X_1 + b_2X_2 + b_3X_3$, where X_1, X_2, and X_3 are covariates) controlling for the treatment variable and that composite would then be used as the single covariate for the analysis described in this section.

Rosenbaum and Rubin (1983) have proposed the use of propensity scores that can be viewed as a form of a mega-covariate. However, in the analysis that they propose, the covariates are combined to explain the treatment variable, not the outcome. One then matches control and treated units on these derived propensity scores. We urge treating the propensity score as a mega-covariate to determine the direction of bias by the method that we describe below.

How to determine the direction of bias is discussed later in this chapter, but we can briefly summarize the results of that discussion here. First, we need to scale the outcome and the covariate. Normally the treatment's goal is to increase the score on the outcome. However, if the goal were to reduce the score (e.g., reduce addiction), then we would reverse the outcome. Second, the covariate (or mega-covariate) is scaled to correlate positively with the outcome variable when the treatment variable is controlled. If the "treatment" difference on the covariate is negative (the control group mean is greater than the treatment group mean), we refer to the program as *compensatory*, and if the difference is positive (the treated units outscore the controls), we refer to the program as *anticompensatory*. This empirically based definition of "compensatory" may conflict with the political or philosophical definition of the intervention. For instance, a program could be designed as compensatory with the goal of helping those who are disadvantaged, but the evaluation may use as a control group those who are even farther behind. So the evaluation study would be anticompensatory even though the program was designed to be compensatory.

We can now state the likely direction of bias for statistical equating as well as matching. If the program is compensatory, the effect of the program is likely underestimated. If the program is anticompensatory, the effect of the program is likely overestimated. The rational for this rule is presented later in this chapter.

It may happen that there is little or no difference between the treatment and control group means on the covariate. By little or no difference, we mean not only no statistically significant difference but also that the estimated effect size of the difference is very small. If this was to happen and matching was not used, the finding of no difference would be an important fact that would deserve prominence in the discussion of the internal validity of the evaluation. If there were a very small difference between treatment groups on the covariate, the problems with statistical equating discussed in this chapter would likely be minimal. Matching tries to make the groups exactly the same on the covariate by discarding a good deal of the data to make it seem as if there is no difference on the covariate. As was explained in Chapter 4, matching creates the illusion, not the reality, of group equivalence.

ILLUSTRATION OF THE BIAS IN STATISTICAL EQUATING

In this section, we show that the problems that we found in Chapter 4 also apply to statistical equating. We present an intuitive explanation of how the method of statistical equating works. We shall see that despite its statistical sophistication, statistical equating is very similar to matching.

Earlier, we created a quasi-experiment in which the same persons were measured at two times. We use in this chapter the same data that we used in Chapter 4. To review, four dice are rolled, as described in Chapter 1. To compute a pretest score, we sum four dice to create 500 treatment participants and then sum four dice with a 4 added to the scores of the 500 controls. To compute the posttest, we save two of the pretest dice and roll two dice and again we add four to treatment participants' scores. Thus, the mean of the lower or treated group is set at 14 at both times and 18 for the upper or control group. The standard deviation is 3.42 for both groups and times. The theoretical size of the gap at both times is 1.17 standard deviation units. The basic statistics are presented in Table 4.1. (How the full data set can be accessed is described in Appendix A.)

We first look at the pretest difference and see that it is –4.01, which is a very large difference. Because the difference is negative (the controls outscore the treated units), the intervention is said to be compensatory.

We first fit parallel regression lines that are shown in Figure 5.1. The pooled slope equals .519 (very close to the theoretical value given the parameters of the simulation of .5). The measured difference in elevation between the two regression lines (the vertical distance) is a measure of the treatment effect. The method of statistical equating uses the regression slope within groups to forecast the change between the different treatment groups. Because the lines are parallel, the vertical distance between the lines is the same for all values of the covariate. Using multiple regression, the estimate

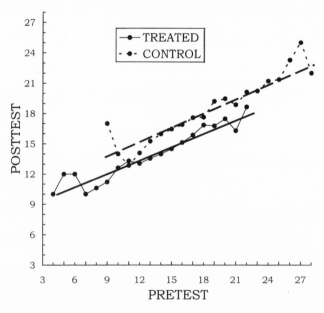

FIGURE 5.1. Parallel regression lines for treatment and control groups fitted by statistical equating (multiple regression).

of the "treatment" effect is −1.72 and is highly statistically significant [$t(997) = -8.00$, $p < .001$]. This estimate is virtually identical to the estimate that we obtained from matching (presented in Chapter 4). Due to sampling error, it is, however, slightly less than the theoretical value of −2.0.

In this simulation, the true treatment effect was set to 0, but statistical adjustment would have produced an "effect" of nearly 2 units, about the same as matching but perhaps more misleading than matching because all of the data were used (rather than just the matched cases).

Ironically, statistical equating fails because it takes too seriously the problem of regression toward the mean. The method begins with a 4-point difference between the two groups at the pretest. Given regression toward the mean and the fact that the variances are the same at both times, a naive view of regression toward the mean is that the gap between groups should narrow. If the two groups were nonrandom samples from one population, then the regression toward the mean would imply that the gap between groups should narrow. However, the groups are not drawn from the same population. Because they are drawn from two different populations with two different means, they are not regressing to the same mean. So, given how the simulation was constructed, the expectation is that the gap between groups should not widen over time.

A little mathematics might improve comprehension here. In our simulation, we assumed that the means and the variances are stationary over time. The formula for the degree of regression toward the mean from Table 2.1 in Chapter 2 is

$$M + r(X - M)$$

where M is the overall mean of the pretest and the posttest, and r is the correlation between pretest and posttest, pooled within groups. If we take this formula and apply it to both the treatment group and the control group and then subtract, we have

$$r(M_T - M_C)$$

which equals the forecasted posttest difference. Given that the actual difference is $M_T - M_C$, the bias in the statistical equating method for the simulation example equals

$$(1 - r)(M_T - M_C)$$

The weaker the correlation between the pretest and the posttest, the greater is the bias in statistical equating. Note that in the above example $M_T - M_C$ equals -4.00 and r equals $.5$, making the bias equal to -2.00, very near the estimated value of -1.72.

DIRECTION OF BIAS

Some sort of statistical equating is necessary because the groups are not randomly formed, and so it is reasonable to expect the means to differ even were there no treatment effect. The fundamental plausible rival hypothesis is that of selection. Any mean difference in the outcome is due to two different sources: selection and a treatment effect. When we adjust the outcome using the covariate (i.e., statistically "equate"), we attempt to remove the effect of the selection component in the outcome.

Figure 5.2 illustrates what usually happens when statistical equating is used. Unlike what we did in the simulation example, we

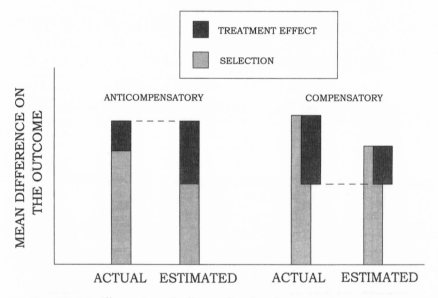

FIGURE 5.2. Illustration of effects of underadjustment for anticompensatory (left diagram) and compensatory programs (right diagram) on mean difference on the outcome between the treatment and control groups (represented by the dashed line); the total effect (the selection plus treatment effect) is the same for the true effect and the estimated effect.

allow for a real treatment effect in the data. Each of the two graphs in Figure 5.2 contains the posttest difference between group means partitioned into two parts: the treatment effect (the dark box) and the selection effect (the lightly shaded box). For both graphs, the mean difference between treatment and control groups on the outcome variable is designated by the dashed horizontal line. For the graph on the left, the effects of selection and treatment are in the same direction. This would be an example of an anticompensatory program: those who are already advantaged, or perhaps deserving, are given a program to help them (e.g., gifted education). For the graph on the right of Figure 5.2, the selection and treatment effects are in the opposite direction. The treatment effect is indicated by a lightly shaded box. This is an example of a compensatory program.

Although researchers are always hopeful that adjustment is successful, the likely effect of statistical equating is underadjustment; that is, the size of the estimated selection effect using the covariate is smaller than the true selection effect. The justification of this expectation is presented below; for the moment, we consider just the effects of this underadjustment, as illustrated in Figure 5.2. For the evaluation of anticompensatory programs, programs in which the treated units outperform the controls, there are overestimates of effects. To see this, consider the left diagram in Figure 5.2. Underadjustment results in an underestimate of the selection effect and an overestimation of the treatment effect.

The right diagram in Figure 5.2 illustrates the effect of underadjustment for compensatory programs—programs in which the controls outscore the treated units on the pretest. Because selection effects are underestimated, the treatment effect is underestimated.

It is theoretically possible for overadjustment[2] to occur: the selection piece of the posttest is overestimated. When this happens, the effects of compensatory treatments are overestimated and anticompensatory treatments are underestimated. However, we believe that overadjustment is atypical for reasons that we now elaborate.

Although statistical equating is likely to produce a less biased estimate of the treatment effect than not adjusting at all, it usually does not fully equate the groups. The reasons for this chronic underadjustment are relatively complex, and so we must explain them in some detail. The fundamental reason for bias in the estimate of the treatment is the failure to measure and control for the variable

---

[2]Campbell and Erlebacher (1970) were mistaken in their claim that the underadjustment always occurs. We are grateful to Lee J. Cronbach, who persuaded both of us that we were wrong.

that is used to assign persons to treatment groups. Judd and Kenny (1981) refer to this variable as the *assignment variable*, and other discussions of this issue refer to the *omitted variable* problem.

Let us first imagine that the covariate is the assignment variable. So, for instance, persons might select themselves into a drug-treatment program based on their motivation to no longer be addicted: the more motivated enter the program. However, the measure of motivation inevitably contains errors of measurement, and measurement error in the covariate almost always results in underadjustment (for the exceptions see the discussion below on when equating works; see also Cappelleri, Trochim, Stanley, & Reichardt, 1991). What measurement error in the covariate does is to lower the slope or steepness in the effect of the covariate on the outcome. Measurement error in the covariate is said to *attenuate* regression slopes. The reader should examine Figure 5.1 again and this time imagine the slopes being steeper (remembering to keep the slopes going through the point $\{M_X, M_Y\}$ in each group). It can be seen that the gap between the two lines narrows. The presence of measurement error results in an overestimation of the treatment effect for anticompensatory programs and underestimation of compensatory programs.

Various methods for accounting for the biasing effects of measurement error have been developed. One method is to correct the slope by what is called a correction for attenuation: the slope is divided by the reliability of the covariate.[3] Another method is to compute estimated true scores, using a formula very similar to the one that we developed in Chapter 2. The details of this approach are described in Reichardt (1979) and Judd and Kenny (1981).

The most common approach to measurement error in a predictor variable is to have multiple measures of the covariate and so the covariate is treated as a latent variable. A structural equation modeling program (AMOS, CALIS, EQS, or LISREL) is then used to remove the biasing effects of measurement error.

We can understand the biasing effects of measurement error in terms of regression toward the mean. The covariate is used to predict the outcome, and prediction always involves regression toward the mean; the degree of regression is, in essence, measured by the correlation between the covariate and the outcome. However, the

---

[3]Other corrections to the slope have been proposed (see Reichardt's common-factor correction in Cook & Campbell, 1979); however, as we discuss later, these corrections are more simply understood as variants of change score analysis.

measurement error in the covariate artificially lowers the correlation between the covariate and the outcome, and so the degree of
regression toward the mean is overestimated.

Measurement error is just part of the underadjustment problem. A more serious problem is that the covariate may not be the
assignment variable. Recall that the assignment variable is the
variable that brings about the nonrandom assignment of persons
to conditions. The degree of bias in the estimate of the treatment
effect depends on the assignment variable causing the outcome
variable after the covariate is controlled. In Figure 5.3, we have
drawn a causal model in which the assignment variable causes the
treatment variable and the covariate. If the covariate mediates the
effect of the assignment variable on the outcome (so that there is
no direct effect from the assignment variable to the outcome),
there is no bias in the estimate of the treatment effect. This direct
effect is represented in Figure 5.3 by the arrow with the dashed
lines.

However, there is bias if the assignment variable affects the
outcome directly. Whether it is underadjustment or overadjustment depends on two effects: the effect of the assignment variable
on the covariate controlling for the treatment variable, and the effect of the assignment variable on the outcome controlling for the
treatment variable and the covariate. Generally these two effects
are in the same direction (Judd & Kenny, 1981). Although this is
not guaranteed, it would be much more likely to occur when the

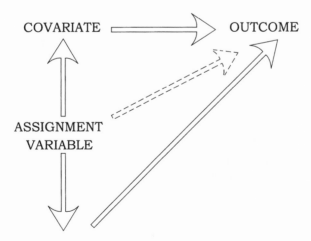

FIGURE 5.3. Model of selection underlying statistical equating.

covariate is a pretest measure. It would seem unlikely that the assignment variable has one effect on the pretest and a different effect on the posttest. If the effects are in the same direction, there is underadjustment; if the effects are in the opposite direction, there is overadjustment. We think it likely that the effects are in the same direction, and so the effects of compensatory programs are likely underestimated and the effects of anticompensatory programs are overestimated. Besides, even in a situation in which there is overadjustment, measurement error typically adds to underadjustment and so can counterbalance overadjustment due to omitted variables (Reichardt, 1979, p. 172).

We suggest the following procedure for researchers who attempt adjustment using a covariate. We first assume that a larger score on the outcome means a "better" outcome. If not, then we reverse the outcome so that larger scores mean less of something bad. We next scale the covariate so that its relationship with the outcome is positive. Then we measure the mean difference on the covariate between treatment groups. If the difference is positive and so the treated units outscore the controls, then the consequence of underadjustment is likely a positive bias: the intervention effect is overestimated. If the difference is negative and so the controls outperform the treated units, then the consequence of underadjustment is a negative bias: the intervention effect is underestimated. This bias may lead to the mistaken conclusion that a program was harmful when in actuality it has no positive benefit or only a small benefit. Understanding the likely direction of bias is essential when using statistical equating. We return to this topic later in this chapter.

WHEN STATISTICAL EQUATING WORKS

In elaborate detail, we have explained the bias that occurs when statistical equating is used. There are, however, three major situations in which statistical equating is effective.

The first such case is a randomized experiment: persons are randomly assigned to treatment groups. For a randomized experiment, statistical adjustment is unnecessary in terms of internal validity, but it may be beneficial through an increase of power. Even though statistical equating results in a slight adjustment of the treatment effect, there is no need to worry about the biasing effects of omitted variables and measurement error in the covariates in randomized experiments. The central concern in randomized experiments is that the covariate should be strongly correlated with the outcome. The success of statistical equating in randomized experiments has led some to think that it is also effective in quasi-experimental evaluations. A major point of this chapter is that this is a mistaken belief.

The second case also requires knowledge of the assignment process. For the regression discontinuity design (Campbell & Thistlethwaite, 1960; Cook & Campbell, 1979; Trochim, 1984), the researcher knows what variable is used to form groups. The variable used to equate groups is the very same variable on which persons were assigned to groups. So, for instance, Mark and Mellor (1991) were interested in the effect of being laid off from work on a "hindsight bias," the mistaken belief that the person knew that the layoffs were coming. Because seniority is used to determine who would be laid off and who would not be, it is the assignment variable. Mark and Mellor (1991) found less hindsight bias in laid-off workers.

A key assumption of the regression discontinuity design is that the functional relationship between the covariate and the outcome is known. Generally, the relationship is assumed to be linear, but nonlinear effects can be estimated and tested. We also note that measurement error in the assignment variable is not problematic. The defining feature of the design is that we know what variable is used to assign persons to treatment groups. The interested reader should consult Trochim (1984) for more details concerning the design.

The third case is one in which the assignment variable is systematic, not random, but does not correlate with the outcome. So in essence the assignment is random, at least with respect to the outcome. Earlier in this chapter, we discussed treating the covariate as an outcome. If such an analysis reveals "no treatment effect" on the covariate, then we can have confidence that the assignment is essentially random with respect to the outcome variable. We must realize that finding no treatment effect on the covariate does not guarantee that the assignment process is essentially random. It may be that the assignment variable causes the outcome but not the covariate. This would be less plausible if the covariate were a pretest measure of the outcome.

ALTERNATIVES TO STATISTICAL EQUATING

There is a totally different approach to adjustment or equating groups. Statistical equating concerns finding the right variables and properly estimating their slope with respect to the outcome variable. An alternative approach is just to accept that there is nonrandom selection and then try to measure its effect using a parallel measure that is not affected by the intervention. Then this selection estimate is subtracted from the difference between groups on the outcome variable. The type of statistical analysis that results is called *change score* analysis. Instead of analyzing the posttest by itself and using the pretest as a covariate, one analyzes the change score or the posttest minus pretest.

Change score analysis, unlike statistical equating, presumes that the difference between treatment groups is not attenuated over time due to regression toward the mean. Statistical equating carefully and precisely estimates the amount of regression toward the mean within treatment groups and uses it to forecast between-group change that may be inadequate, as we have seen. Change score analysis presumes that there is no regression toward the mean between groups despite the fact that there is regression within groups. Regression toward the mean is inevitable, but all scores need not regress to the same mean.

When we look at group means on a pre- and posttest, we see if the gap between groups changes over time. When we look at mean changes over time, we implicitly use change score analysis in determining whether there are treatment effects. Change score analysis seems to be the natural method to use largely because we naively do not consider regression toward the mean.

Despite its strong intuitive appeal, change score analysis has been savagely criticized in the literature on a number of grounds (e.g., Cohen & Cohen, 1983). One criticism is that the method is naive. Change score analysis implicitly weights the pretest by 1, whereas statistical equating weights the pretest in a statistically optimal fashion. Another criticism is that the method is inefficient. The variance of change scores is virtually always greater than the variance of the posttest minus the pretest adjusted by statistical equating. Finally, change score analysis has been criticized as very unreliable. We return to some of these criticisms in Chapter 6.

In spite of these criticisms, in the last 10 or so years, change score analysis has made an amazing comeback (Wainer, 1991). We quote from Rogosa, Brandt, and Zimowski (1982): "In summary, the often cited deficiencies of the difference score . . . are more illusory than real" (p. 735). So, despite these statistical deficiencies, change score analysis has a place in quasi-experimental evaluations. The method has regained the respect that it rightfully deserves.

Change score analysis, like any other analysis, is not without its pitfalls. Its key assumption is that the selection effect in the posttest exactly equals the selection effect in the pretest. There may be an interaction between selection and maturation: the gap between the groups may be widening over time. Simple change score analysis presumes that no such interaction exists. If the gap widens over time, the effects of compensatory programs are underestimated and anticompensatory program effects are overestimated. The opposite happens if the gap narrows. We now discuss two analytic approaches to the plausible rival hypothesis of selection by maturation interaction.

Standardized change score analysis (Judd & Kenny, 1981; Kenny, 1975a) can be used to control for some forms of the selection by maturation interaction. The logic of this analysis is that the selection by maturation interaction implies a change in variance: there is increasing variance over time. By equating variances at the pre- and posttest by standardization, the plausible rival hypothesis of selection by maturation would be rendered less plausible. Following Judd and Kenny (1981), we do not recommend a separate standardization of the pretest and the posttest, but rather the following strategy. The raw pretest is not subtracted from the posttest; instead, the pretest is first multiplied by s_Y/s_X, where s_X and s_Y are the pooled within-group standard deviations of the pre- and posttest, respectively.[4] [The pooled within-group variance equals the mean square error from a regression analysis in which the treatment and covariates (not the pretest) are entered to predict the pretest and posttest.]

Kenny and Cohen (1980) have suggested a more complicated but likely more valid factor than s_Y/s_X by which to multiply the pretest. The method is fairly complicated, and so we just outline the approach. There must be a set of covariates, demographic variables such as age, gender, and ethnicity (but not a pretest). Separate regressions are run for the pre- and posttest with these demographic variables as predictors. The change in the coefficients of the demographic variables then specifies the amount of change needed to weight the pretest.

Because assignment to groups is not random, we cannot be certain about the degree of bias in any analysis. Quasi-experimental

---

[4]Recall from Chapter 2 that s_Y/s_X is the perfect-correlation line. In essence, this weighting of the pretest acts as if the pretest–posttest correlation were perfect, and so it forecasts that there would be no between-group regression toward the mean.

analysis requires assumptions, and the violations of those assumptions become plausible rival hypotheses.

An obvious question presents itself: when should the researcher use statistical equating, and when should he or she use change score analysis? We have some advice on this issue. First, statistical equating should never be used by itself. If it is to be used, there should be corrections for measurement error in the covariates. Also, the analyst must assume that the pretest true score is the assignment variable. Change score analysis requires the assumption that the pre- and posttest are parallel measures and that selection is on a variable that does not change over time. Thus, the difference between groups at the pretest can be used as a measure of selection effects. If change scores are used, consideration must be given to the selection by maturation interaction.

Ever since Lord (1967) pointed out that statistical equating and change score analysis yielded different answers (something that came to be called *Lord's paradox*), there has been considerable debate over which is the appropriate method for analyzing data from the nonequivalent control group design. The right answer is that neither method is always appropriate, but rather each method is appropriate given different assumptions about the assignment variable and change over time. The major obstacle is that these assumptions cannot be easily tested. Moreover, the assumptions made by each procedure are very strong and so are unlikely to hold.

EXAMPLES

We consider two very controversial examples chosen to attract interest. To soften the political blow of the examples we suggest that politically conservative readers read the first example first and that liberal readers read the second example first. In both illustrations, despite the contrasting political implications, we argue that statistical adjustment results in underadjustment.

Gender Pay Inequity

We turn our attention to what has become a rather contentious issue: gender differences in pay. It is a fact that currently in the United States and many other countries, men earn more than women. Certainly part of the gap in pay is due to discrimination. Some employers have unfairly assumed that women do not need to earn as much as men because they are not the "primary" wage earner. Others have mistakenly assumed that women are less productive than men. The sexist assumptions and practices of employers have been extensively catalogued.

However, the entire pay gap is not due to gender discrimination. Although not universally true, in many occupations men have more seniority than women. Moreover, men enter some jobs with greater qualifications. Because of these differences, researchers have attempted statistically to equate men and women on various background characteristics. Although such equating is likely to produce a less biased estimate of the gender difference (though this is not totally guaranteed), it likely only partially "equates" the groups. The reasons for this underadjustment are measurement error in the covariates and other variables omitted from the analysis.

The likely bias is that of underadjustment. Because men typically (though not always) score more highly than women on most of the covariates and because the covariates likely correlate positively with income, the likely case is that gender gap in income due to discrimination is overestimated.

Ethnic Differences in Intellectual Ability

While those who prefer to be politically correct might be very upset with the previous example, they should like this one. Research has consistently shown that there are differences between whites and African-Americans in the United States on standardized achievement tests. (If the example makes the reader uncomfortable, it might help if Asians are substituted for whites and whites for African-Americans.) In attempting to explain this difference, researchers have attempted to equate the groups statistically by controlling for parental socioeconomic status and other parental variables. Although including these variables in the analysis reduces the ethnic difference, differences usually persist between whites and African-Americans in standardized achievement tests. The presence of these differences has led some to conclude that there is a genetic difference between the two groups. It seems to us that a regression artifact caused by insufficient equating is the likely source of most, if not all, of the remaining difference. There is likely measurement error in these covariates, and not all of the covariates have been measured and controlled.

We believe that the bias in statistical equating for ethnic differences in achievement and intelligence testing is almost certainly underadjustment. Whites generally score more highly than African-Americans on the covariates. Their parents have better jobs, have higher incomes, and have more education. It has been well documented that these socioeconomic differences are positively correlated with achievement test scores, and so controlling for these covariates only partially adjusts for differences between the two groups. The most likely case is that the advantage of whites over African-Americans in "equated" standardized achievement is overestimated.

CONCLUSION

We hope that the strong political content of the foregoing examples has not distracted the reader from the major point of the chapter. Statistical adjustment (i.e., "controlling" the effect of the pretest in multiple regression), like matching, while often improving the comparison between nonrandomly formed groups (vs. totally ignoring the covariate), does not guarantee that the comparison is unbiased. Moreover, we should expect that the correction would be only partially successful. Statistical equating creates the illusion and not the reality of equivalence.

It is ironic that statistical equating produces regression artifacts in that statistical equating focuses on the concept of regression toward the mean. In essence, the method uses within-group regression toward the mean to predict the between-group regression. The problem, however, is that often scores in the two groups are not regressing to the same mean but to two different group means. Thus, statistical equating predicts more regression toward the mean than actually occurs (Lund, 1989b).

Although regression toward the mean is inevitable for the entire sample, it is not a certainty for any subset of scores. We need to know why the score is extreme. If the factor that is used to select the score does not change, then the score will not regress to the mean. For the simulation data set, there is no regression toward the mean on the selection variable of group membership. There is regression toward the mean on other variables (people are changing), but those variables were not used to assign person to groups.

Should the researcher attempt statistical adjustment? If done with care and thought, adjustment usually improves the validity of the difference between groups. However, adjustment rarely, if ever, provides exactly the right answer. Statistical adjustment usually results in underadjustment, and the researcher needs to expect that the estimated treatment effect is likely biased. For compensatory programs the bias tends to be negative, and for anticompensatory programs the bias tends to be positive. If statistical adjustment is the planned strategy, one needs to think critically about the set of potential covariates. Once they are selected, one should measure them as reliably and as validly as possible. One should consider strategies to minimize measurement error and to control for its biasing effect through a latent variable analysis (i.e., structural equation modeling). However, one needs to realize that statistical equating is unlikely to provide an unbiased estimate of the treatment effect.

We have argued in this chapter that statistical equating usually underadjusts for differences on the covariate. Chronic underadjustment is very often ignored when conclusions from the research are drawn. Warning labels should routinely accompany estimates from quasi-experimental evaluations. We suggest the following wording:

> The use of this method to adjust for covariates in the absence of randomization usually results in underadjustment. Because the treated (control) group outscores the control (treated) group on the set of covariates, the effect of the intervention likely is larger (smaller) than it appears.

Different messages would be printed depending on the direction of the difference between treatment groups on the covariate and the covariate's correlation with the outcome. If there were multiple covariates, a mega-covariate would be computed. In the absence of warning labels, we urge the reader to determine the likely direction of bias. Ideally, the research report ought to contain enough information to enable the reader to make such a determination. However, sometimes the reader may have to contact the investigator to obtain the requisite details. Such information is absolutely essential for the intelligent comprehension of the analysis. By knowing the likely direction of bias, conclusions derived from the statistical analysis can be qualified in a scientifically defensible manner. The failure to understand the likely direction of bias when statistical equating is used is one of the most serious difficulties in contemporary data analysis. In modern society we have warnings on car mirrors, over-the-counter medicines, and music CDs (compact discs). Why should we not have warnings in computer software?

In the next chapter, we continue our discussion of change. But there we focus not on measurement of program change but on measurement of individual change.

6

Regression Artifacts in Change Scores

In the previous two chapters, we have seen that the analysis of change scores, posttest minus pretest, is an alternative to matching or covarying on the pretest. In this chapter we consider change scores. More has been written about regression toward the mean and change scores than any other topic in the regression toward the mean literature. Because of this extensive focus, there has been considerable psychometric work on the topic. So this chapter violates a prime principle of this primer: reliance on graphical presentation over algebraic formulas. Despite the many formulas in this chapter, we present an intuitive understanding of their meaning.

The focus in this chapter is the measurement of change in individuals and the related issue of the identification of persons who have changed more. In the previous three chapters, we considered the issue of the causes of change, which we, as well as Cronbach and Furby (1970), view as very different from the question of the measurement of individual change.

In this chapter, we make the oversimplifying assumption that errors of measurement are not correlated over time. An error of measurement refers to an irrelevant source of variation. When these irrelevant sources are the same or similar over time, errors of measurement are correlated. An example of correlated measurement error would be using the same achievement test at two times. It is likely that lucky guesses at one time will be repeated at a second time, thereby creating correlated errors. We refer the reader to other sources for the complications brought about by correlated measurement errors (Cronbach & Furby, 1970; Williams & Zimmerman, 1977). Although many of the formulas in this chapter change, their basic features persist.

We need to make clear that before change scores are computed, the same variable is measured at both times. It is worth quoting directly from Lord (1958):

> The test no longer measures the same thing when given after instruction as it did before instruction. If this is asserted, then the pretest and posttest are measuring different dimensions and no amount of statistical manipulation will produce a measure of gain or of growth. (p. 440)

A related issue is that the metrics of the two measures should be the same. So, if the metric of the pretest is the percent correct, the metric of the posttest should also be the percent correct of items drawn from the same pool. If they are not, then "change" is like subtracting "apples from oranges." Sometimes data transformations are needed to preserve metric equivalence (Judd & Kenny, 1981).

CORRELATIONS WITH CHANGE SCORES

Consider a pretest X, a posttest Y, and the change between the two $Y - X$. We begin with a statistical fact. If the variance in the measures is stationary ($s_X^2 = s_Y^2$), then the correlation of the pretest with change cannot be positive and is almost certainly negative. It is a simple matter to show that if the variances of X and Y are the same, then the correlation of change, or $Y - X$, with initial standing, or X, is

$$-\frac{\sqrt{(1-r)}}{\sqrt{2}}$$

where r is the correlation between X and Y. Given stationary variance, the correlation between change and initial standing can never exceed 0.

In general the correlation of change with the pretest is

$$\frac{rs_Y - s_X}{\sqrt{(s_X^2 + s_Y^2 + 2rs_Xs_Y)}}$$

Because the denominator must be positive, the sign of this correlation depends on the numerator. For the correlation to be positive,

s_X/s_Y must be less than r. Because r cannot be greater than 1, the variance must be increasing over time for there to be any possibility of a positive pretest–change correlation.

When variances are equal and the correlation is less than 1, a negative pretest–change correlation is an inevitable consequence of regression toward the mean. To see this, reconsider Figure 1.8 from Chapter 1. It is a Galton squeeze diagram in which the left vertical axis refers to the pretest and the right to the posttest. In that figure, there is about a .5 correlation between X and Y, the means and variances are stationary, and there are 500 cases. The slope of lines connecting the two vertical lines reflects the average change scores. The Galton squeeze diagram clearly shows that large pretest scores are associated with declines in scores, or negative change scores, whereas low pretest scores are associated with increases, or positive change scores. This resulting pattern implies a negative correlation between initial standing and change.

Whereas change tends to correlate negatively with initial status, change tends to correlate positively with final standing. Thus, the posttest tends to correlate positively with a change score. (See the Galton squeeze diagram in Figure 1.8.) A good rule of thumb, given generally positive correlations, is that measures taken at the pretest tend to correlate negatively with change scores whereas scores measured at the posttest tend to correlate positively with the change score. (This rule follows from the principle of proximal autocorrelation that is discussed extensively in Chapters 8 and 9.)

Beginning with an article by Wilder (1950), there has been some interest in what has been called "the law of the initial value." In essence, this literature is concerned with the correlation between the pretest and the degree of change. Some have claimed that the correlation is positive, and others have claimed that it is negative. As we and countless others have previously shown, the correlation must be negative if the variance does not increase over time. Moreover, very often, even if the variance increases over time, the correlation between initial standing and change may still be negative. Thus, the so-called law of the initial value is not a law of nature but a mathematical necessity and a restatement of regression toward the mean.

Sometimes researchers correlate change, or $Y - X$, not with the pretest or the posttest but with the average of the two, or $(X + Y)/2$. The sign of this correlation depends on only the change in the variance over time: if the variance is increasing, then the correlation must be positive; if the variance is decreasing, then the correlation must be negative; if the variance does not change, then the correlation must be 0. Thus, the correlation between change and average of the two scores is not very interesting substantively.

The correlation of change with the average does have another, less obvious, use. It can be used to test statistically whether variances computed on the same persons are changing over time.

RELIABILITY OF CHANGE SCORES

It has been long known that change scores have surprisingly low reliability, even if the components that make up the change score have high reliability. If we denote r_X as the reliability of the pretest, r_Y as the reliability of the posttest, and r as the correlation between the pretest and the posttest, the reliability of the change score can be shown to equal

$$\frac{s_X^2 r_X + s_Y^2 r_Y - 2rs_Xs_Y}{s_X^2 + s_Y^2 - 2rs_Xs_Y}$$

which, when the variance is stationary ($s_X^2 = s_Y^2$), reduces to

$$\frac{r_X + r_Y - 2r}{2(1-r)}$$

Moreover, if the two reliabilities are equal ($r_X = r_Y$), the above further reduces to

$$\frac{r_X - r}{1 - r}$$

So, if the variances are equal, the reliabilities of the measures are .85, and the test–retest correlation is .75, then the reliability of change scores is a paltry .40. (Generally .6 is thought of as the minimal value for acceptable reliability, and some would even consider this unacceptable.) It may seem counterintuitive, but as r increases the reliability of change scores actually decreases. So, if $r = .80$ and $r_X = r_Y = .85$, the reliability of change scores is only .25. (Note that r should be less than or equal to the square root of r_Xr_Y.)

This low reliability of change scores seems like a serious problem, and for this reason some have recommended never computing change scores. Why use as an outcome measure something that has a reliability in the 40's? Researchers began to realize that there was less reason to worry after Overall and Woodward (1975) showed that in some cases the lower the reliability of change scores, the greater the power to detect intervention effects. The embarrassingly low reliability of change scores is currently not viewed as a problem by most psychometricians (Collins, 1996), a view that we share.

The Overall and Woodward (1975) paper is very controversial. Many psychometricians have attempted to resolve the paradox of greater power with lower reliability, and some have argued that Overall and Woodward (1975) were mistaken. We find the paper by Nicewander and Price (1978) to be the best resolution of the controversy. They noted that a change in reliability of a measure does not necessarily imply anything about the power of the test. If reliability is increased because the error variance decreases and the true variance remains the same, then an increase in the reliability of the change scores does increase the power of the test. However, if the reliability increase is due to an increase in the true score variance independent of the treatment effect, then the increased reliability lowers power. The interested reader should consult Fleiss (1976), Humphreys and Drasgow (1989), and Sutcliffe (1980) for further discussion of the Overall and Woodward (1975) paper.

THE MEASUREMENT OF CHANGE

To illustrate the different measures of individual change, we now develop a simple example: imagine that you are president of a small company and you have 12 employees for whom there are productivity data for the current year (Y) and the past year (X). These hypothetical data are contained in Table 6.1. The mean across the 12 persons changes very slightly over time, going from 11.43 to 11.46; the variance increases from 2.96 to 3.43; and the correlation over time is .549.

Raw Change

You, as the company president, want to reward the two workers who improved the most. That would seem to be a simple task: you compute the change scores and see whose change scores are the largest. Using this criterion, the winners are shown in bold in the fourth column of Table 6.1: persons J and L. These two persons would seem to be the clear winners, but alternative definitions of change yield different winners.

TABLE 6.1. Hypothetical Performances and Four Different Measures of Changes of 12 Employees

Person	X	Y	Method I	Method II	Method III	Method IV
A	12.1	12.1	.0	.253	−.340	.020
B	11.3	12.9	1.6	**1.525**	.868	1.088
C	12.2	11.1	−1.1	−.806	−.949	−.722
D	9.3	10.6	1.3	.407	**1.696**	.850
E	11.7	8.8	−2.9	−2.811	−1.621	−1.948
F	11.2	12.0	.8	.685	.509	.545
G	12.1	10.3	−1.8	−1.547	−1.257	−1.194
H	11.4	9.0	−2.4	−2.493	−1.219	−1.615
I	12.1	13.3	1.2	1.453	.271	.831
J	10.1	12.1	**2.0**	1.434	1.660	**1.337**
K	15.3	15.2	−.1	**1.462**	−1.961	.008
L	8.4	10.1	**1.7**	.439	**2.341**	**1.105**

Note. Boldface indicates the two persons who improved the most for that method. Method I, raw change score; Method II, residualized change score; Method III, "backward" residualized change score; Method IV, estimated true change score.

Residualized Change Score

Because of the inevitability of regression toward the mean, it has been suggested that there should be a correction in the change score for regression toward the mean. Note that the "raw change winners" were both below the mean at the pretest, and so some of their gain is, at least in some sense, inevitable. The standard adjustment is to compute what has been called a *residualized change score* (Dubois, 1957). In essence, this measure "seeks to determine what the observed change would have been if everyone had started out equal on X" (Rogosa et al., 1982, p. 741). Its formula essentially takes the residual from the regression analysis to make predictions and so can be viewed as $Y - Y'$, where Y' is the predicted posttest score from the regression equation (see Chapter 2). The standard formula for residualized change scores is

$$Y - b_{YX}(X - M_X) - M_Y$$

The residualized change score has been in use for decades, and like any good idea this measure has been reinvented (Heimendinger & Laird, 1983).

Using this definition of change, the winners are now persons

B and K, two different winners from those produced by the raw change analysis. Note that person B's score at the pretest is very near the pretest mean and so very little of that person's change is attributed to regression toward the mean. Both of the raw change winners were below the mean, and so much of their change is attributed to regression toward the mean. But note that person K's raw score actually declines over time. Yet that person is seen as the one with the second greatest residualized change increase. How can this be? Person K scored very high on the pretest, 2.13 standard deviations above the mean. We would expect person K to decline by about a standard deviation, and that person did decline—but not nearly as much as would be expected, given regression toward the mean.[1]

There is yet another way to measure change. Why use past to predict future? Why not use the future to predict the past? The argument is in essence to measure change backward. The formula for the predicted pretest, given the posttest, is $b_{XY}(Y - M_Y) + M_X$. Because the measure $X - X'$ is "backward," we should multiply it by -1. The resulting measure of time-reversed residualized change is

$$-X + b_{XY}(Y - M_Y) + M_X$$

This measure, though mathematically permissible, can be difficult to interpret. It represents the difference from where the person started to where it is forecasted that the person should have started. Perhaps it could be said to measure the "you have come a long way baby" distance. Using the backward residualized change, the winners are D and L. Both of these persons have posttest scores near the mean; hence, there is little regression in those scores and low pretest scores, and so they have "come a long way." As far as we know, this measure has never been presented before.

To understand better the differences between these two measures of residualized change, we illustrate the computation of one case in some detail. Before we begin, note that raw change is computed as $Y - X$ whereas residualized change equals $Y - Y'$, where Y' is the predicted Y given X. Comparing the two formulas, note that Y' replaces X in the formula, and so the variable Y', in a sense, takes on the role of a "pretest."

Consider the illustration in Figure 6.1. The scores of one per-

---

[1]True-score corrections to residualized change are possible, but they do not change the rank order of the scores (Cronbach & Furby, 1970).

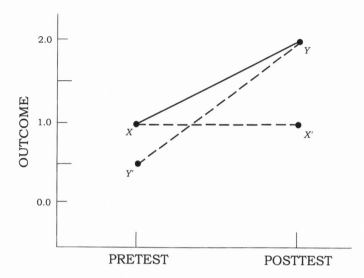

FIGURE 6.1. Residualized change backward and forward in time.

son are presented. That person is 1 unit above the mean on the pretest (X) and 2 units above the mean on the posttest (Y). The raw change is given by the difference in the levels of the two scores and is indicated in Figure 6.1 by the solid line going from X to Y.

We assume that the regression coefficient in both directions is .5 and the means of X and Y are equal. We have also graphed the expected posttest given the pretest or Y' using the formula presented in Chapter 2. To show the change, we have placed the expected posttest or Y' as a "pretest." We have connected the posttest (Y) and the expected posttest given the pretest (Y') by a dashed line. The gap between the posttest and expected posttest, Y – Y', is the measure of residualized change from pretest to posttest. We see that because the person is above the mean at the pretest, this measure of residualized change (1.5 units) is somewhat larger than the raw change measure (1 unit).

However, we can also look at how much "change" would be expected going from the posttest to the pretest, that is, looking backward in time. So we examine change from the expected pretest or X' to the actual pretest or X. To show the change, we place the predicted pretest at the posttest. This backward residualized change measure is X' – X. For the illustration in Figure 6.1, there is no expected change in this direction. The dashed line is flat because both X and X' equal 1. Given that the person is fairly extreme at the posttest, the score would be expected to regress toward the mean.

Residualized change is a temporally asymmetric measure and has what the physicists call an *arrow of time*. That is, change is very different when we are looking in one direction (from the past to the present) than when we are looking in the other direction (from the present to the past). We return to the issue of temporal asymmetry in Chapter 10.

Estimated True Change

Cronbach and Furby (1970) described yet another measure of change that they credited to Lord (1956, 1958, 1963) and McNemar (1958), and we sometimes refer to this as the Lord–McNemar measure of change. This is a very complicated measure of change that we break into a series of steps. First, X and Y are used to predict the true scores of X. In Chapters 2 and 3, we discussed how an observed score can be used to predict a true score. What is different here is that two observed scores are used to predict a true score and so the true score must be estimated from a theoretical multiple regression. The resulting estimated true score is a composite of the two observed scores. The estimated true score for X, denoted as X_T', can be estimated by

$$X_T' = (X - M_X)\frac{r_X - r^2}{1 - r^2} + (Y - M_X)\frac{s_X(r - r_X r)}{s_Y(1 - r^2)} + M_X$$

where r_X is the reliability of X. Next, X and Y are used to predict the true score of Y. That predicted score, denoted as $Y_{T'}$, is

$$Y_T' = (Y - M_Y)\frac{r_Y - r^2}{1 - r^2} + (X - M_X)\frac{s_Y(r - r_Y r)}{s_X(1 - r^2)} + M_Y$$

The Lord–McNemar measure of change is then defined as

$$Y_T' - X_T'$$

and it can be called *estimated true change*. As the pre- and posttest reliabilities approach 1, the estimated true change measure approaches the raw change measure.

Table 6.1 presents the estimated true change measure for the 12 employees. We have assumed that the reliability of both the pre-

and posttest is .85. The meaning of reliability in this context would be the theoretical correlation with an alternate measure of productivity. Despite all of the computation, we see that the winners are persons J and L, the very same winners as with raw change, a rather typical result. The variability of the estimated true change is less than the variability of raw change scores, but the two usually correlate very highly with each other. In fact, if the reliabilities and the variances of the pre- and posttest are the same, the correlation of raw and estimated true change is necessarily 1.

As was shown in Chapter 3, true-score estimation reduces the variability of measures. This same shrinkage is found when two measures are used to estimate the true score. Shrinkage in prediction is a theme that we revisit in Chapter 10.

There are even more complicated ways to measure change. Bayesian methods can be used to estimate the rate of change per unit time. We do not consider those methods here; however, the interested reader can consult Rogosa et al. (1982) for an introduction to this approach.

So who should get the bonus? Should we give it to J, L, D, K, or B? No one person is in the "top two" for all four of the definitions. The choice of the winner depends on how change or improvement is defined. The raw change winners can claim that they increased the company's profits more than anyone else. The residualized change winners can argue that they brought more profits than were "expected," either expected given the past or expected given the present. The estimated true change winners can claim that they are making more true or real profits for the company, not more measured profits.

The "forward" residualized change score would seem to provide a very reasonable statistical estimate of change. It states how much change there is after controlling for regression toward the mean. There are, however, problems with the measure. First, as we have shown, it may yield some strange winners. For the example in Table 6.1, one of the residualized change winners actually declined! This type of anomaly may make it a difficult measure to use with a statistically naive audience. Second, residualized change scores violates the principle of time reversal that we discuss again in Chapter 10. Third, Rogosa et al. (1982) review several statistical difficulties with the measure.

Because there are different answers about who changed most, this does not mean that it is arbitrary how change is measured. Just because change is difficult to measure does not mean that it should not be measured. We get different answers because we measure change using different definitions of change. It should not be surprising that different questions have different answers.

CORRELATES OF CHANGE

The focus of this chapter is the *measurement* of change and not the understanding of the causes or correlates of change. In this section, we consider the problem of the attribution of change. We have presented four different measures of change: raw change, residualized change, "backward" residualized change, and estimated true change. Which of these measures should be correlated with other variables? This is a complicated and very controversial issue, with psychometricians quite divided over it (e.g., compare Collins, 1996, to Humphreys, 1996). We now offer some advice on this issue.

One practice that should be discouraged is that of correlating residualized change with other measures. If residualized change scores are desired, it is almost always better instead to employ statistical equating by using multiple regression; that is, instead of residualizing the outcome variable (i.e., removing variance due to the pretest) before performing the analysis, one should treat the pretest as a covariate in the statistical analysis. The use of residualized change in studies of the correlates of change is fraught with difficulties of improper degrees of freedom, inefficiency, and bias.

Following Cronbach and Furby (1970) and others, we advise the reader not to correlate estimated true change with other variables. Recall that this measure usually correlates highly with raw gain, and so raw gain can be used instead of estimated true change.

We are then left with raw change and statistical equating as measures of change. These two measures were discussed in Chapter 5. We adapt that discussion and consider how to measure the effect of Z on Y controlling for X. In essence, statistically equating throws X in the regression equation and statistically adjusts for its effect. In change score analysis, the outcome is adjusted by subtracting the pretest from the posttest.

In deciding how to "control" for the pretest, we need to have an understanding of why it is that X is correlated with Z, besides causing it. As in Chapter 5, we now develop a model of selection in which there is an unknown, confounding variable, called the assignment variable, that creates the correlation between Z with X

and Y. In the previous chapter, we considered two alternative models of selection.

In one model of selection, the assignment variable is assumed to cause X and Z, and X is presumed to cause Y. However, the assignment variable has no direct effect on Y, and so X is assumed to mediate the effect of the assignment variable on Y (see Figure 5.3). One major concern of this analysis is that if it is true X, not measured X, that mediates, then ignoring measurement error in Y likely leads to underadjustment. This model of selection underlies treating the pretest as a covariate.

In the second model of selection, the assignment variable is assumed to cause both X and Y to the same extent. We also have no causal relationship between X and Y. To remove the biasing effect of selection in the posttest, the pretest is subtracted from it to remove the effects of the assignment variable. If such a model of selection were true, some sort of change score analysis would be valid. Again we refer the reader to the discussion of change scores in the previous chapter as well as that by Judd and Kenny (1981; see especially Chapter 5 therein).

In Chapter 9, we consider yet another model of selection. As in the previous model there is stationarity, in that the assignment variable has the same effect on the pretest and posttest. However, in this model there is change in the assignment variable. In Figure 9.2, the assignment variable is designated as Z.

We wish to emphasize one key point. All too often researchers statistically equate or compute change scores without thinking through a model of selection. We urge a careful consideration of the process before the statistical analysis is undertaken. By choosing a model of selection, the researcher has decided what pattern of regression toward the mean will occur.

CONCLUSION

Our primary purpose in this chapter is the measurement of individual change, not the attribution of the causes of change. This would seem to be an easy topic, but it is not. The measurement of change scores has been and continues to be a very controversial topic. For many years statisticians and psychometricians have criticized it as naive and ignorant. They have complained about its low reliability. It became so bad that one oft-cited article had the title, "How We Should Measure 'Change'—or Should We?" (Cronbach & Furby,

1970). In recent years, change scores have experienced a revival and there has been increasing acceptance of measuring change, even raw change scores. Ironically, one of the key papers resurrecting change scores had as its first author a student of Cronbach (Rogosa et al., 1982), one of the coauthors of the paper that sent change scores reeling for a generation.

We offer the following advice about the measurement of change.

First, if change scores are computed, it is inadvisable to correlate them with initial status. That correlation would likely be negative and must be negative if the variances do not increase. Given the principle of proximal autocorrelation (see Chapter 8), it is a very dangerous practice to correlate change with a measure that is time dependent, either the pretest or the posttest. Given positive correlations, "pretest" measures tend to correlate negatively with change and "posttest" measures correlate positively.

Second, the reliability of change scores tends to be very low. Although researchers should strive for measuring variables with as much reliability as possible, the low reliability of change scores is not inherently a problem.

Third, if researchers are trying to calculate those who change the most and those who change the least, they need to consider the various definitions of change and choose the one that makes the most sense for their own purposes.

Fourth, if the researcher is trying to make attributions to the causes of change, this chapter is largely irrelevant. It is better to consult Chapters 5 and 9 as well as other sources (Judd & Kenny, 1981). The researcher should determine what is the most plausible model of selection; that is, the researcher needs to understand why the pretest is correlated with the causal variable. Depending on what assumptions are made about selection, the researcher may well use change scores, but it is inadvisable ever to use residualized change scores or estimated true scores.

It may seem surprising that something as simple as "change" is so complicated. Much of the complications and difficulties stem from regression toward the mean. Three major edited volumes (Collins & Horn, 1991; Gottman, 1995; Harris, 1963) have been written on change, and likely more ink will continue to be spilled regarding this subject. One theme that we return to in the conclusion of this primer (Chapter 10) is that simple questions usually require complicated statistical methods. Change is not nearly as simple a concept as it might naively seem. In Chapter 10, we return to the concept that simple ideas often require complex statistical analysis.

The next two chapters return to the discussion of quasi-experimental treatment evaluation. The common theme of both chapters is what happens when there are more than two time points. In Chapter 7 we consider time-series data, and in Chapter 8 we discuss multiwave studies.

7

Regression Artifacts in Time-Series Studies[1]

In time-series data, a single person or unit is measured at more than one point in time. Typically, the unit is a governmental unit such as a state or a country, but sometimes it is a person who receives some sort of behavioral intervention. Regression artifacts plague the interpretation of program effects in time-series data, and in this chapter we consider three illustrations of these problems. We also develop a method to measure and correct for these regression artifacts in time-series data.

To determine regression toward the mean we need to know the correlation between adjacent data points. The measurement of correlation for time-series data is relatively complex. To measure the correlation between adjacent data points, the data must be lagged. A series and its lagged series are presented below:

$$6, 7, 8, 6, 5, 4, 4, 5, 7, 8$$
$$| \quad | \quad | \quad | \quad | \quad | \quad | \quad | \quad |$$
$$6, 7, 8, 6, 5, 4, 4, 5, 7, 8$$

A lagged correlation is called an *autocorrelation*. The graph of these correlations against lag length is called an *autocorrelogram*. We pre-

---

[1]Much of this chapter was originally published in Campbell (1996). We are most grateful for permission from Elsevier Science to reprint this material.

sent formulas for computing autocorrelations in Appendix B. Besides the traditional formula, we also present a more complicated but less biased formula for the lag-1 autocorrelation that is given by Huitema and McKean (1994).

The analysis of time-series data is complicated by the presence of trends and cycles. A trend might be that the series is generally increasing over time. A cycle might be an annual cycle such that observations are greater in the summer than the winter. In this presentation we do not consider cycles, but a complete discussion of time-series analysis would need to consider them (Judd & Kenny, 1981; McCain & McCleary, 1979). For the last illustration in this chapter, we consider a trend, a constant change as a function of time. We downplay these complications because we wish to focus on the effect of regression toward the mean.

A myriad of models can be used to explain the autocorrelational structure of time-series data (Judd & Kenny, 1981; McCain & McCleary, 1979). To simplify the discussion, we generally assume in this chapter that the correlational structure is a first-order autoregressive structure: each time point causes the next time point. If we denote a as the autoregressive coefficient, the lag-k autocorrelation equals a^k. Characteristic of this structure is that correlations decline the longer the time lag, and for long lags the autocorrelation is essentially 0.

We now consider three extended examples from previous analyses of the first author. All three illustrations focus on the fact that interventions are often triggered by an extreme observation, making regression toward the mean a serious concern.

THE CONNECTICUT CRACKDOWN ON SPEEDING

We introduce the problem by a condensed discussion of an example that has been presented in previous papers (Campbell, 1969a; Campbell & Ross, 1968). It is perhaps the best known illustration of the interrupted time-series design. Figure 7.1 shows annual automobile traffic fatalities in the state of Connecticut for the years 1951 through 1959. At the beginning of 1956, the governor of the state, Abraham Ribicoff, introduced an extremely severe enforcement of automobile speed limits. The following year he claimed great success "with the saving of 40 lives, a reduction of 12.3% from the 1955 motor vehicle death toll, we can say the program is definitely worthwhile." He was reporting on just the years

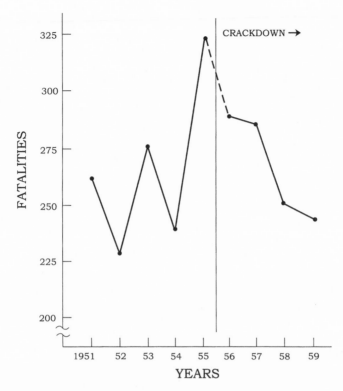

FIGURE 7.1. Annual Connecticut traffic fatalities from 1951 to 1959. Adapted from Campbell (1996). Copyright 1996 by Pergamon Press. Adapted by permission of Elsevier Science.

1955/56 (the dashed line in Figure 7.1), which do indeed show a decline.[2]

When we look at the extended series, we start doubting the governor's claims, because the 1951/52 and 1953/54 drops are just as large and occur prior to the crackdown on speeding. The most striking year-to-year shift is the 1954/55 gain. An examination of the governor's announcements at the beginning of the crackdown

---

[2]Abraham Ribicoff died while this primer was being completed. Despite the Connecticut crackdown being a classic regression artifact, it was still reported in his obituaries that "Connecticut's highway deaths continued to drop, and Mr. Ribicoff's stature soared" (*Hartford Courant*, February, 23, 1998, p. A8).

makes it most plausible—indeed, virtually certain—that the sharp 1954/55 gain caused the crackdown. Given a chance component in the rates for each year, shown by the unexplained fluctuations, it becomes highly likely that the 1955 peak was, in part, caused by a year-specific chance component operating so as to make it exceptionally high. For the following years, it would be unlikely that the year-specific chance component would be as large. Thus, a return to the general trend would be expected, and this is indeed what is found. Thus, the 1955/56 drop is very plausibly only a regression artifact, produced by selecting a peak in an unstable time series as the point to initiate the crackdown (thus anchoring the analysis on the 1955 data), rather than being caused by the crackdown itself. Asking the question: "Why was the crackdown introduced then?" alerts us to the role such dramatic reforms play in the larger system, as well as the role of focal public social indicators such as traffic fatalities.

The regression artifact interpretation is quantifiable. In this primer, we develop a simple forecasting strategy. As is to be seen below, our approach is consistent with the regression toward the mean forecasts made in other chapters. Another approach is to estimate ARIMA time-series models (McCain & McCleary, 1979). We consider estimation using the more complicated ARIMA models in the last section of this chapter.

As in most time-series modeling, one would need a long time series (e.g., at least 50 preintervention time periods). To measure the amount of regression toward the mean, we compute the lag-1 autocorrelation (see Appendix B). This autocorrelation can be used to estimate the expected value for the first postintervention data point using the following formula:

$$r_1(Y_{pre} - M_Y) + M_Y$$

where r_1 is the lag-1 autocorrelation, Y_{pre} is the preintervention data point, and M_Y is the mean of the preintervention data points. Using the terms defined in the previous chapter, we are suggesting a form of residualized change. In general, the prediction for the kth observation after the intervention is

$$r_k(Y_{pre} - M_Y) + M_Y$$

where r_k is the lag-k autocorrelation. If we can assume that the model is first-order autoregressive, then r_k can be estimated by r_1^k, where r_1 is the lag-1 autocorrelation. (The parameter of a first-order autoregressive model can be estimated by the lag-1 autocorrelation.)

We evaluated this approach by simulating time series that had at least 50 time points before the intervention. We found that by not using the two time points just before the point of intervention we produced relatively unbiased estimates of the lag-1 autocorrelation and the mean. With these values we estimate the observation after the intervention by using a varient of a formula presented in Chapter 2 of $r_1(X_{pre} - M_Y) + M_Y$.

There are much too few data from the Connecticut crackdown study to try this approach. However, if we assume that the autoregressive coefficient is .4 and use the mean of the series before the intervention, we find that the predicted decline is .4(324 − 260) + 260, which equals 285.6, a number that is virtually identical to the actual number of fatalities for the first year after the intervention: 284. We repeat that this illustration is more suggestive than definitive because we guessed but did not estimate the lag-1 autocorrelation.

THE OFFSET EFFECT OF PSYCHOTHERAPY

Next, let us examine a still subtler version of the same problem in the analysis of the cost and benefits of psychotherapy in prepaid medical insurance programs. Jones and Vischi (1979) have reviewed studies in which mental-health services were given to patients at a specific point in time and in which there was a reduction in their demand for all types of medical services, the often-claimed *offset* effect. Thus, psychotherapy is seen as a cost-effective use of resources because its cost is *offset* by reduced use of medical services.

In Figure 7.2, we present a hypothetical time series in which the cost per month is graphed for about a year and a half. At some point the person has a psychotherapy visit (the solid vertical line), and we can then examine from that point, both backward and forward, whether costs are declining. The solid line of Figure 7.2 illustrates the most typical pattern of data presented and the 20% decline typically found. However, although the graph is based on hypothetical data, it is representative of results from many studies. Olbrisch (1977, 1980) has criticized such evidence on the grounds that transiently high users of other medical services were referred to psychotherapy, or they may have sought it out themselves in a transient period of high disturbance cosymptomized also by high med-

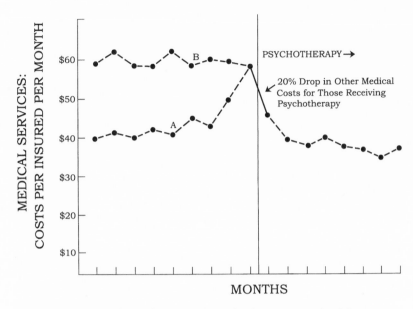

FIGURE 7.2. Hypothetical effect of psychotherapy in a health maintenance organization; the solid line corresponds to effects noted in several
studies, and the dashed lines represent two possible pretrends. Adapted
from Campbell (1996). Copyright 1996 by Pergamon Press. Adapted by
permission of Elsevier Science.

ical demands, that is, a regression artifact. Kogan, Thompson,
Brown, and Newman (1975) have also interpreted their own data
as showing regression artifacts.

From the records of the health insurance programs (or health
maintenance organizations, HMOs), it should be possible to provide extended pretreatment time-series data testing this criticism
even though such series have rarely been examined. All studies
agree that the psychotherapy participants had on the average been
exceptionally high users of medical services immediately prior to
therapy being provided. The issue relevant to Olbrisch's argument
is whether or not this high usage was an atypical increase, in which
case a return toward the mean would be expected without therapy.
Figure 7.2 illustrates such a history in the line labeled as A. Alternatively, if those receiving therapy had a sustained record of high
usage, followed by the 20% drop, as illustrated by line B of Figure
7.2, then the regression artifact interpretation seems to be ruled
out. The time series becomes impressive evidence of genuine im-

pact of psychotherapy (unless someone comes along with a more plausible rival hypothesis).

Among the hundred or so data sets presented by Jones and Vischi (1979), there are only two that present more than one time period prior to psychotherapy. These two are presented in Figures 7.3 and 7.4. Unfortunately, for proponents of offset argument, both strongly support the regression artifact interpretation. The decline in medical services is just as evident before as it is after the onset of psychotherapy. The declines shown are thus most plausibly interpreted, at least in substantial part, as pseudodeclines.

Let us expand the regression artifact explanation. The graphs in Figures 7.2, 7.3, and 7.4 are not in real or calendar time, but rather in time units for each patient, before and after psychotherapy. The many individual time series have been averaged after being coaligned around the onset of psychotherapy. Each patient series of medical usage is full of stochastic fluctuations. The regression artifact interpretation requires that assignment to psychotherapy occur at a high peak of patient complaints and use of diagnostic tests. If

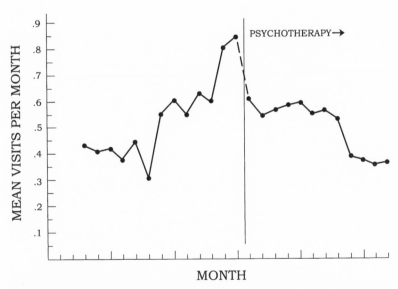

FIGURE 7.3. Mean physician visits per month of 426 patients, before and after psychiatric intervention. Adapted from Campbell (1996; after Jones & Vischi, 1979, p. 54, Table 18, based on data from Patterson & Bise, 1978, supplemented by a personal communication from Bise). Copyright 1996 by Pergamon Press. Adapted by permission of Elsevier Science.

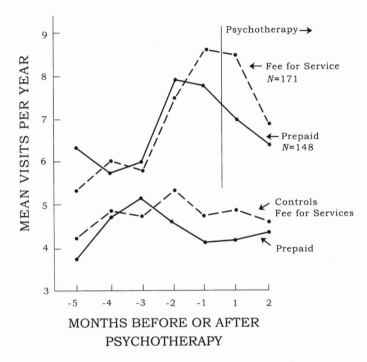

FIGURE 7.4. Mean outpatient visits by year, before and after initiation of psychotherapy. Adapted from Campbell (1996; after Jones & Vischi, 1979, p. 54, Table 18, based on data from Kogan et al., 1975). Copyright 1996 by Pergamon Press. Adapted by permission of Elsevier Science.

the time series of demand is indeed full of instability, with chance peaks, then it follows that subsequent demand (as well as previous demand) would tend to average more nearly the level of the individual's own norm. Because hundreds of individual records have been averaged, the resulting curves are smooth and so fail to show the instability that the individual series would show.

Although the analysis of a single series is informative, the addition of control groups, such as those in Figure 7.4, can greatly strengthen causal inferences. A different type of control group would also be useful. Thus, if one searched the nontherapy cases in the program from which Figure 7.3 comes for the first single month of usage above some high value (e.g., .80 in the figure), and plotted the 12-month span surrounding these and averaged 500 such case instances, one might have a portrait of a pure regression artifact due to selecting an extreme point to initiate therapy. One could also do without a control group, computing the autocorrelation at various lags for all patients for extended times lacking a psychotherapy intervention, and then use their average to predict values both before and after the onset of psychotherapy.

The 20% offset-effect results have been reported triumphantly in billion dollar arguments as to whether or not fees for psychotherapy should be reimbursed by health insurance and whether or not HMOs should provide it. With these data being used in such a high-stakes arena, it seems possible that selective reporting has been involved. Given that one of the earliest studies (Kogan et al., 1975) set the precedent shown in Figure 7.3 of using multiple time periods before the onset of psychotherapy, why have virtually all of the subsequent studies omitted this feature? The records were certainly there to be examined. Was it because these multiple pretreatment values provided a picture hard to explain, and one that undermined the causal interpretation of the cost reduction? If such analyses were done, were they suppressed by voluntary self-censorship, because of the researcher's economic stake in the cost-reduction interpretation? We would hope that economic interests would not affect the presentation of data from quasi-experiments. We return to the topic of advocacy versus science in Chapter 10.

In terms of the economic arguments about psychotherapy coverage in health insurance, it is the costs, not the number of visits, that are important. Because these are available from the archival records, monetary costs should have been used in such analyses in addition to, or instead of, the number of visits. The importance of the problem requires a more comprehensive evaluation of available data. One wonders if only the number of visits has been presented because visits show larger effects than do costs? Because the types of visits that provoke referral to psychotherapy are probably those low-cost visits in which no medically diagnosable ailment is found, the regression artifact pattern might be relatively less sharp for a time series of costs.

In HMOs such as Kaiser-Permanente, group insurance programs had at one time made psychotherapy coverage available as an optional feature. Such HMOs have more recently changed their programs in this regard, with precisely datable changes. This situation makes possible testing the claim that adding psychotherapy to a company's health insurance plan will reduce its overall costs. Have such time series been run and yielded no offset effect? Or have they even found an increase in costs? That this rich resource of records has perhaps only been used (e.g., Follette & Cummings,

1967; Cummings & Follette, 1968, 1976) to produce persuasive misleading results is highly deplorable.

TIME SERIES OF HIV TREATMENTS IN CLINICAL TRIALS

The following illustration is wholly conjectural. Its inclusion is felt justified by the potentially great importance of interrupted time-series quasi-experimental designs in research on possible cures, a potential not now being exploited. The regression artifacts that might sometimes be involved are computable, which provides a way of distinguishing them from genuinely therapeutic effects.

In the last 25 years, the norms for testing new pharmaceutical therapies have completely shifted to randomized trials. Overall, this shift is to be applauded, but it has been so overdone that credible evidence from nonrandomized clinical trials is now being neglected. It is now time to devote methodological attention to improving nonrandomized clinical trials by making them more effective in clarity of causal inference. Randomized trials are costly, time consuming, and awkward to implement. Further, innumerable therapeutic packages need exploring. Interpretable nonrandomized clinical trials with encouraging effects should be used to pilot-test therapies, discovering those promising enough to warrant expensive randomized trials. In addition, even though new medicines are always initially in short supply (so that most of the appropriate needy are untreated anyway, and thus randomized trials serve to decrease the number of untreated, not increase it), designated untreated control groups feel deprived and vocal opposition to such experiments is generated.

As a prototypical methodological model, we might look into the research that established the efficacy of penicillin, for example, the 5-day cure of syphilis introduced around 1940. It is our understanding that no randomized trials were used. Instead, the quasi-experiments were totally convincing. Patients whose blood tests had regularly shown spirochetes for years and years suddenly tested free of them after one such treatment. Were we to graph the results for a single patient, they would probably have looked like the data in Figure 7.5.

Replicated over dozens of clinical tests and rarely refuted in later applications, the clinical and scientific communities were completely convinced, and rightfully so. Large-magnitude effects can be very convincing (Abelson, 1995), and so randomized clinical trials would have been superfluous. Probably graphs like that in

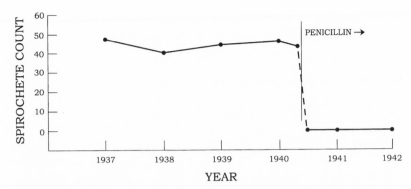

FIGURE 7.5. Hypothetical time series of spirochete counts for a single patient administered penicillin. Adapted from Campbell (1996). Copyright 1996 by Pergamon Press. Adapted by permission of Elsevier Science.

Figure 7.5 were not prepared, nor was there any methodological emphasis on keeping the method of assay comparable across times for a single patient and across patients. For less dramatic cures, clinical practice needs to be improved for clarity of causal inference.

The method that we propose is most appropriate for long-standing pathology indicators that have been repeatedly measured prior to the onset of treatment. Our method is not appropriate for acute flare-ups, as has been demonstrated in the two previous illustrations. For example, it would be inappropriate for testing cures for fevers, inasmuch as every cure would be found "effective" due to regression toward the mean.

To make the discussion more concrete, consider the controversy over "Compound Q" at the Sixth International Conference on AIDS in San Francisco, as reported in a *New York Times* (Saturday, June 23, 1990, p. 24) Editorial entitled "Tests of New AIDS Drug Assailed at Parley":

> Martin Delaney, who heads Project Inform, the San Francisco AIDS organization that is coordinating the trials, said the 46 patients in the experiment had improved significantly over the first four months of taking the drug. . . . Before participants in the trial started taking Compound Q, they were losing immune system cells called CD-4 cells at an average rate of one cell every three days. While taking the drug, he said, they gained an average of two cells every three days. . . . But there is no control group in the Project Inform experiments; each patient's condition is simply compared to his condition before starting to take the drug. Many researchers are extremely critical of this

approach. . . . Mr. Delaney has said his organization's unconventional trials were necessary because people with AIDS were already taking the drug in larger doses on their own. Mr. Delaney's announcement today was attacked immediately by Dr. Arnold Relman, the editor of *The New England Journal of Medicine*. The two were on a panel on clinical trials. "You don't know and we don't know whether this is just a flash in the pan," Dr. Relman said. While he approves the expansion of clinical tests to get drugs to fatally ill patients sooner, Dr. Relman said, he is "opposed to irrational and uncontrolled experiments!" Other researchers at the conference said these data were not enough to make the case that the drug had been helpful, and criticized Mr. Delaney for not providing more information. Dr. Relman said it was wrong for Mr. Delaney to give selective bits of data to the public very early in the experiment, before review of the data from independent researchers.

We have not examined the details of Delaney's data. They may indeed not have justified his claims. But they also could have been compelling, as was the penicillin-for-syphilis case, without a control group.

Let us assume, first, that he had repeated measures on the CD-4 T-cell (or T-lymphocyte) level for 5 or so months prior to the introduction of Q-therapy (or X-therapy, as in Figures 7.6 and 7.7), and for a similar number of months afterward; second, that the introduction of therapy was *not* timed as a response to a particularly low measure; third, that during the 10-month period no other therapy was introduced. (A constant background of other remedies during this 10-month period would not be invalidating.) The outcome of single patients might look like that shown in Figure 7.6. Such an outcome is compelling insofar as there are no plausible rival explanations for the change in slope. Most of laboratory experimentation in the physical and biological sciences similarly lacks a control group. The preintervention points serve as a form of control group.

In Figure 7.6, the treatment seems to have been successful in slowing the rate of decline or reversing it, but the results are uncompelling for single cases (in contrast with the penicillin–syphilis example). Combining those of Delaney's 46 cases for which there are a sufficient number of pre- and postmeasures and producing an average time series (aligned in terms of months before and months after treatment, rather than calendar time) could produce a smooth and convincing plot, such as in Figure 7.7.

No doubt we already know a great deal about the frailties of CD-4 T-cell tests. For example, should all of them be early morning

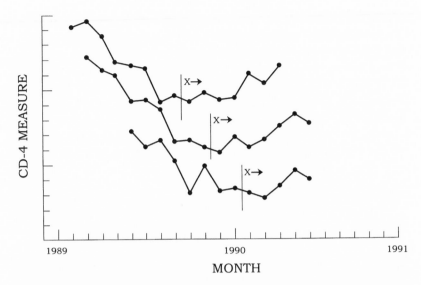

FIGURE 7.6. Several hypothetical individual time series of a CD-4 T-cell measure. Adapted from Campbell (1996). Copyright 1996 by Pergamon Press. Adapted by permission of Elsevier Science.

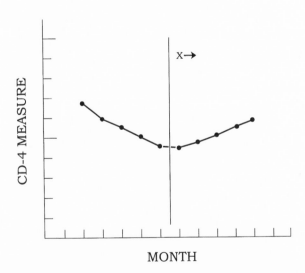

FIGURE 7.7. Hypothetical averages of many individual time series of the CD-4 T-cell measure, reorganized into months before and after introduction of X-therapy. Adapted from Campbell (1996). Copyright 1996 by Pergamon Press. Adapted by permission of Elsevier Science.

fasting blood samples? Do doctors with HIV patients obtain frequent enough blood tests? Are there seasonal trends liable to produce pseudoeffects? It might be that usable data could be obtained from existing patient records. More likely, the U.S. government [e.g., National Institute of Allergy and the Infectious Diseases (NIAID), National Center for Health Statistics (NCHS), Centers for Disease Control (CDC)] could provide supplemental funding to several thousand clinicians with HIV patients so that such time series would be available on a number of indicators against which to test new therapies clinically.

The most likely source of a pseudoeffect in a case such as Delaney's Q-therapy comes from a combination of an erratic time series of measures and the initiation of treatment in response to an extreme measure. If the CD-4 T-cell measure shows the sort of instability illustrated by the three patients in Figure 7.8, and if treatment was usually introduced right after an extremely low measure, then on average the immediately following measures would show a less extreme departure from the general trend even if the treatment had no effect. Figure 7.8 illustrates this for an average of many cases, realigned after the initiation of our imaginary X-therapy.

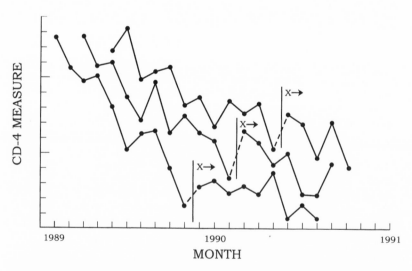

FIGURE 7.8. Hypothetical individual time series in which there is no true reversal of trend but in which X-therapy is always introduced after an erratic high score. Adapted from Campbell (1996). Copyright 1996 by Pergamon Press. Adapted by permission of Elsevier Science.

As we have already discussed, the shape of this pseudoeffect curve can be estimated from a time-series autocorrelogram of the correlations of differing lags based upon records in which no treatment was introduced. In Figure 7.8, a first-order autoregressive process has been assumed, with a coefficient of .5 and a linear descending trend. That is, from the extreme point just before treatment was introduced, the adjacent points before and after are halfway back to the basic trend line; for those 2 points away, for which $r = .5 \times .5 = .25$, the regression to the trend has been 75%; for those 3 points away, for which $r = .5 \times .5 \times .5 = .125$, the regression toward the trend has been 87.5%; and so on.

From Delaney's case records we should be able to decide whether the onset of treatment was, in a given case, precipitated by an extreme measure. Moreover, from his and other records, we should be able to estimate typical CD-4 T-cell trends for HIV-positive patients in the absence of treatment, as well as the autoregressive coefficients. These should enable us to predict the degree of "regression to the trend" expected as an artifact alone. From the news story, Delaney seems to be claiming a reversal of direction far beyond that explainable by the regression to the average trend of Figure 7.9.

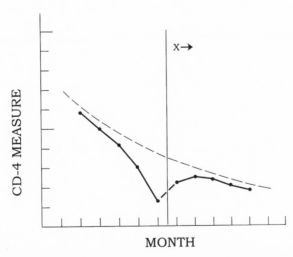

FIGURE 7.9. Hypothetical example of the average of many time series with a pseudoremission result (lighter dashed line represents the true trend and bold line represents pseudoremission result). Adapted from Campbell (1996). Copyright 1996 by Pergamon Press. Adapted by permission of Elsevier Science.

For prospective quasi-experiments of this type, there are additional precautions that could be taken. After the decision to introduce X-therapy, one could routinely wait several measurement periods before starting it; or one could introduce such a delay only in cases in which the decision was made after an extreme measure, as judged by the expected trend for such cases and that patient's own measurement series. Of course, the ethics of such an intervention plan would need to be evaluated. But, if the study were ethical, it would be a way to evaluate the effectiveness of new drug therapies. We consider statistical adjustments in the next section.

ARIMA MODELING AND REGRESSION ARTIFACTS

The often recommended approach to time-series modeling is ARIMA (autoregressive integrated moving average) modeling (Judd & Kenny, 1981; McCain & McCleary, 1979). This modeling approach can estimate and test a wide range of models. A good introduction to these methods is presented by McCain and McCleary (1979). Although these methods can estimate elaborate models of serial dependency (the correlation between adjacent observations), it is not clear that they can adequately deal with the regression artifacts in the data that we have discussed in this chapter. Because regression artifacts likely produce biased estimates of the mean and the autoregressive coefficient, intervention effect estimates may be biased.

A major practical difficulty in time-series analyses is that correction for serial dependency requires estimates from the data but the statistical theory on which these estimates are based often require relatively large samples (at least 50 data points). However, typically in intervention analysis the sample size is very small. It is not known how well the large-sample method works with small samples.

We conducted a computer simulation to determine the sensitivity of ARIMA modeling to both regression artifacts and small samples. We created 1,000 time-series data sets, each with 20 observations: 10 pretreatment and 10 posttreatment observations. The model that we simulated was a first-order autoregressive model. To create a regression artifact, the treatment was always introduced after a 2 standard deviation increase in the time series, which means that the observation before the intervention had to be 2 standard deviations greater than the population mean of the pretreatment observations. We refer to this as a nonrandom introduction of the

treatment. Figure 7.10 presents an illustration of one of the time series with such a treatment. It can be seen there that the intervention
occurs immediately after an extreme observation, much like some of
the real examples discussed previously in this chapter.

The simulated model has four parameters: the autoregressive
coefficient (set to .5); the mean of the pretreatment observations
(set to 5.0); a treatment effect (set to −1.0, making the mean of the
posttreatment observations 4.0); and the variance of the random
component added to the observations (set to .75). SAS Institutes's
(1984) PROC ARIMA estimated the parameters of this model.

Table 7.1 presents the basic set of results from this simulation.
We first consider the results from the 500 samples with random in-
troductions of the intervention. We see that the autoregressive coefficient was underestimated, the earlier cited problem of small-
sample bias. However, there is not much bias in the estimate of the
intervention effect.

Alternatively, when the treatment is nonrandomly introduced, the treatment effect estimates are biased. Ironically, the autoregressive coefficient is essentially unbiased but the pretreatment
mean is. Because that mean is biased, the extremity of the preintervention point is underestimated. This underestimation results in
substantial bias in the estimate of the treatment effect, on the order
of half a standard deviation.

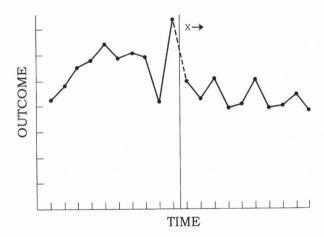

FIGURE 7.10. Simulated time series with an exceptionally large pretreatment observation before the intervention point. Adapted from Campbell
(1996). Copyright 1996 by Pergamon Press. Adapted by permission of Elsevier Science.

TABLE 7.1. Results of 1,000 Trials of a Simulation Using a First-Order Autoregressive Model with 10 Pretreatment and 10 Treatment Observations

| Parameter | Intervention | | |
	Population	Random	Nonrandom[a]
Autoregressive coefficient	.50	.32	.48
Pretreatment mean	5.00	4.96	5.51
Treatment effect	−1.00	−1.02	−1.52
Error variance	.75	.74	.90

[a]Intervention introduced after a 2 standard deviation change and with the preintervention being 2 standard deviations above the mean.

We recommend the following strategy for removing the bias. Two dummy variables are created that code the two observations just before the interventions. One dummy variable equals 0 for all points except the one just before the intervention, and for that value the dummy variable equals 1. The other dummy variable is just like the first, except that the penultimate observation equals 1 and the rest 0. We suggest "dropping" these two observations for the following reason: the observation just before the intervention is likely to be extreme, and the one before that might be extreme in the opposite direction; by eliminating those observations that are likely to be extreme, the mean of the pretreatment observations should be less biased. Limited simulation work has shown that the addition of these two dummy variables results in a much less biased estimate of the intervention effect. These additional dummy variables are necessary to control for the potentially biasing effects of regression toward the mean.

Two degrees of freedom are lost by this approach, and this might be costly if there are few points in the time series. One might think that an alternative approach would be to treat these observations as missing. This, however, is not a viable strategy because the observation just before the intervention is needed to calculate the amount of regression toward the mean expected for observations after the introduction of the intervention.

CONCLUSION

This chapter has presented three extended examples. A common theme is that often the timing of the initiation of the intervention is selected when a time-series observation takes on an extreme value. Given the extremity of the value, we would expect regression toward the mean of the series—and so "improvement" appears to occur. Very often the regression from extremity masquerades as an intervention effect. We have also shown that even sophisticated estimation procedures like ARIMA modeling can be fooled by these regression artifacts.

One advantage of time-series designs is that the biasing effect due to the extremity of the initiation of the intervention can be estimated. If the autocorrelational structure is known, the degree of such regression artifacts can be computed and thus distinguished from a genuine impact of the intervention. Within ARIMA modeling, we recommend introducing dummy variables for the two observations just before the intervention occurs. Such controls are necessary to remove regression toward the mean as a plausible rival hypothesis. Further statistical study is needed to evaluate this and other methods to control for regression artifacts.

In this chapter, we have largely ignored the additional complications of trends and cycles that usually occur in time-series modeling. Moreover, we have assumed that the autocorrelational structure is first-order autoregressive. In principle, we believe that it is still possible to use our approach with these more complicated models. We encourage work in this area.

Another issue is that often there are multiple time series, and how to pool results across many different time series is an important problem deserving of attention. That is, it should be possible to test whether the autocorrelational structure is the same for different units. Problems of small-sample bias need to be considered, because when there are many series it is likely that they are of short duration. Most likely, multilevel modeling can be applied to this problem.

In the next chapter, we explore further the analysis of a form of time-series data. There we have a very short time series, with as few as four time points. However, in this case we have many time series, perhaps hundreds. We shall see that regression artifacts also plague these longitudinal studies.

8

Regression Artifacts in Longitudinal Studies[1]

By *longitudinal study*, we refer to studies in which a large number of units of measurement (e.g., persons or census tracts) are all measured at periodic intervals (e.g., every year) and in which the units are individually identifiable in each period. (A time series—just discussed in Chapter 7—involves few units, often just one, measured at many different times.) The time differences between intervals need not be the same length (e.g., yearly) but often are. For most of the applications in this chapter, units are measured at least four times.

In this chapter, we first consider the correlational structure of longitudinal or multiwave data. Recall that the degree of regression toward the mean depends on the correlation between measures. If we understand the correlational structure, we can predict the degree of regression over time. As an example, we examine the correlational structure over 45 years of measurements of physical attractiveness. In the next section, we consider the mean change or trend lines over time. We are mainly concerned about mean differences between groups formed by matching. We consider in some detail a well-known evaluation of a job-training program. We believe that in this data set regression artifacts create a difference in trend lines.

Generally in this chapter we assume stationarity of parameters; that is, the variance of the variable does not change over time and the correlation across the same lag length is the same for all

---

[1]Much of this chapter was originally published in Campbell (1996). We are most grateful for permission from Elsevier Science to reprint this material.

pairs of variables. Of course, real data do not exactly meet these assumptions, but for pedagogical reasons we oversimplify. For the physical attractiveness example, we do allow for changes in correlation over time and, in fact, it is the change in correlation that is one of the most important aspects of that example.

OVER-TIME CORRELATIONAL STRUCTURE

We begin with the fact that the correlational structure of longitudinal data almost always has a *proximally autocorrelated* structure: adjacent waves of measurement correlate more highly than nonadjacent waves, and the more remote in time, the lower the correlation (Campbell & Reichardt, 1991; Kenny & Campbell, 1989). So the longer the time lag, the lower the correlation. This empirical truism has been found for economic, social-attitudinal, biological, and educational measures. Except for data that are highly cyclical (Warner, 1998), proximal autocorrelation is the norm.

An example of proximal autocorrelation is presented in Table 8.1. The correlation matrix is taken from Humphreys (1960) and consists of grade-point averages measured on 91 students across eight semesters. The data show the typical pattern of decreasing correlations at longer lags: a proximally autocorrelated structure. The average correlation between adjacent waves is .66, between waves separated by two semesters is .61, and between waves separated by three semesters is .58. The data illustrate the typical pattern of proximal autocorrelation. In the remainder of this section, we consider models that would bring about proximal autocorrelation.

TABLE 8.1. Correlations of Grade Point Average across Eight Semesters

X_1	1.00							
X_2	.69	1.00						
X_3	.55	.65	1.00					
X_4	.46	.58	.65	1.00				
X_5	.45	.50	.59	.62	1.00			
X_6	.41	.60	.60	.63	.61	1.00		
X_7	.34	.41	.56	.66	.64	.65	1.00	
X_8	.33	.44	.52	.53	.68	.69	.72	1.00
	X_1	X_2	X_3	X_4	X_5	X_6	X_7	X_8

Note. N = 91. From Humphreys (1960). Copyright 1960 by the Psychometric Society. Reprinted by permission.

Table 8.2 presents four major patterns of correlational structure. In the first pattern, shown in part A of the table, there is an
unchanging variable that creates the correlations between the
waves. If the effect of this unchanging variable, usually called a
trait, is the same at each wave, all of the correlations are the same.
Because the trait does not explain all of the variance of the measures, the remaining variance is denoted as *error*. Quite clearly, this
model does not imply a proximal autocorrelational structure.

**TABLE 8.2. Four Over-Time Correlational Structures (Autoregressive
Parameter Set to .8)**

A. Trait pattern: trait (.70) and error (.30)

X_1	1.000				
X_2	.700	1.000			
X_3	.700	.700	1.000		
X_4	.700	.700	.700	1.000	
X_5	.700	.700	.700	.700	1.000
	X_1	X_2	X_3	X_4	X_5

B. Simplex pattern: state (1.00)

X_1	1.000				
X_2	.800	1.000			
X_3	.640	.800	1.000		
X_4	.512	.640	.800	1.000	
X_5	.410	.512	.640	.800	1.000
	X_1	X_2	X_3	X_4	X_5

C. Quasi-simplex pattern: state (.90) and error (.10)

X_1	1.000				
X_2	.720	1.000			
X_3	.576	.720	1.000		
X_4	.461	.576	.720	1.000	
X_5	.369	.461	.576	.720	1.000
	X_1	X_2	X_3	X_4	X_5

D. Trait–state–error pattern: trait (.50), state (.40), and error (.10)

X_1	1.000				
X_2	.820	1.000			
X_3	.756	.820	1.000		
X_4	.705	.756	.820	1.000	
X_5	.664	.705	.756	.820	1.000
	X_1	X_2	X_3	X_4	X_5

Despite the infrequency of finding this pattern in data, it is nonetheless assumed by many statistical techniques. For instance, repeated measures analysis of variance assumes this structure, as well as many multilevel models. Within the repeated measures literature, the assumption of this correlational structure is called *homogeneity of covariance* or *compound symmetry*.

For the pattern in part B of Table 8.2, the scores change and the resulting structure is said to be *proximally autocorrelated*. This pattern has been called a *Guttman simplex* (e.g., by Humphreys, 1960), but the more common name is a *first-order autoregressive model*. The assumption of the first-order autoregressive model is as follows: a person's score is caused by only the person's score from the prior wave of measurement. The pattern for a first-order autoregressive structure is often assumed for time-series data and is discussed in Chapter 7. If the variables were categorical, a first-order autoregressive model would be a first-order Markov model.

In part B of Table 8.2, there is an autoregressive model with the autoregressive coefficient set at .80. We have assumed perfect reliability (i.e., no error variance). Note that the ratio of correlations at adjacent lags (longer lag correlation divided by shorter lag correlation) is always the same value of .80. In a simplex, each correlation equals the autoregressive coefficient raised to the kth power, where k is the time lag between measurements. If we were to plot the correlation in logarithm coordinates against lag length, the resulting graph would be a straight line.

We refer to a variable that changes in an autoregressive fashion as a *state*. Of course, not all state variables have such a structure, and so we are using the term "state" in a restricted sense of the term. A trait can be viewed as a variable that has an autoregressive coefficient of 1 and an error that has an autoregressive coefficient of 0.

In part C of Table 8.2, we have taken the pattern in part B and added measurement error at each time. The model then contains state and error variance. These correlations are identical to those in part B except that all correlations are multiplied by a common reliability. We still see the general pattern of decreasing correlation over longer elapsed time or proximal autocorrelation. Illustrated here is a very simple first-order autoregressive process plus a time-specific error. The reliabilities have been set at .90, and the autoregressive coefficient has been set at .80. Thus the 1-year lag value is .9 × .8, the 2-year value .9 × .8 × .8, and so on. When measurement error is added onto a simplex, the resulting model is called a quasi-simplex. Real correlation matrices, for example the grade-point average data in Table 8.1, do not look exactly like that in part C of

Table 8.2 because the autoregressive coefficients and the reliabilities change over time.

Given a first-order autoregressive model with measurement error, there is a constraint on the correlation matrix. For four waves of data (1–4), the following should hold: $r_{14}r_{23} = r_{13}r_{24}$. More typical, however, $r_{14}r_{23}$ is somewhat greater than $r_{13}r_{24}$ (Campbell & Reichardt, 1991), something that does not happen for the data in Table 8.1 (only in 40% of the cases is $r_{14}r_{23}$ greater than $r_{13}r_{24}$). So real data characteristically show departures from the first-order autoregressive pattern, almost always in the direction of decreasing decrements with longer lags. Larger correlations than a first-order autoregressive process would show for the longest lags. An example of this structure is presented in part D of Table 8.2. There are two major ways in which that pattern of results can be explained.

First, as discussed by Campbell and Reichardt (1991), such a pattern would be produced if the process were a second-order autoregressive. In this model, the true score is affected by the previous wave and the wave before that. The lag-2 path must be positive to explain the pattern of results that we typically see in data. There is a specification difficulty for this model. For first-order autoregressive models, the lag length need not be specified. Thus, if people were measured every month, every 6 months, or every year, the model is still correctly specified. However, if the model is second-order, the lag length must be correctly specified. If lags should be 6 months and 1 year, then the sample must be measured every 6 months. If however, people are measured every year, the model would contain a specification error. So we judge the second-order model as relatively implausible, as it depends on the length of lag, which is usually arbitrarily chosen.

Second, the trait–state–error model, developed by Kenny and Zautra (1995) and anticipated by Kenny (1975a), can explain this correlational structure. The model is similar to a first-order autoregressive model, but it also includes a trait factor that does not change over time. So unlike the autoregressive model that predicts that eventually the correlation over time is 0, the trait–state–error model predicts that the floor in the lagged correlations is the trait variance.

The trait–state–error model has interesting implications for regression toward the mean. In a state model every individual regresses to the same mean. So, in the long run, we do not expect any initial difference between two persons to persist. In the long run, they would be different, but the direction of that difference would be unpredictable. However, for the trait–state–error model, individuals are not regressing to the same mean but to their own mean. Alternatively, in this model subgroups of individuals are regressing to different subgroup means. So, in the long run, persons become more similar but not exactly similar. Any initial difference would tend to exist later in time, though in a somewhat diminished form.

We generally favor the trait–state–error model over the other models discussed in this section. We do so for the following reasons. First, it is the most general model in that it subsumes all of the previously discussed models, with the exception of the second-order autoregressive model. Second, it makes predictions that are in accord with empirical patterns. As one example, if we were to estimate each of the models implied in Table 8.2 for the data in Table 8.1, the trait–state–error would be the best-fitting model. Also, as Kenny and Campbell (1989) point out, the trait–state–error model can explain why time-series data have relatively low autocorrelations (Huitema, 1985) and longitudinal data have large ones. Third, it is a rich theoretical model. Many researchers have debated whether constructs are traits or states. This model turns that debate into an empirical question.

The trait–state–error model is useful in considering the analysis of treatment variables. The model has been implicitly assumed in Chapters 4 and 5. There we assumed that individuals are not all regressing to a common mean, implying stable differences between persons or between the social groups of which they are members. The trait factor can reflect differences between groups as well as persons. In Chapters 4 and 5, the simulation model assigned persons to treatment groups on the basis of a trait factor, group membership. As Kenny (1975a) discussed, selection can also occur on the state or error factors. Moreover, intervention effects can change the trait (permanent effects), error (temporary effects), or state (decaying effects) factors.

It need not be assumed that the trait resides in the person or the person's genes. Stable differences between persons may also be due to different, but stable environments. Also the trait factor may change, but the rate of change may be too slow to detect given the interval between the first and last wave of measurement.

The differences between the four models in Table 8.2 are graphically illustrated in Figure 8.1. We label the models in the figure as A through D to parallel the four models in Table 8.2. For each model, the autocorrelation is graphed as a function of lag length. As discussed in Chapter 7, this type of graph is called an *autocorrelogram* in time-series research. For each model, the different sources of variance are illustrated by dashed lines. For state vari-

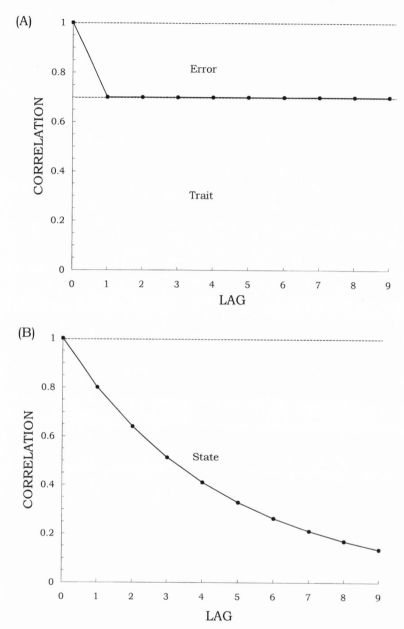

FIGURE 8.1. Autocorrelational structures of four different models (A–D).

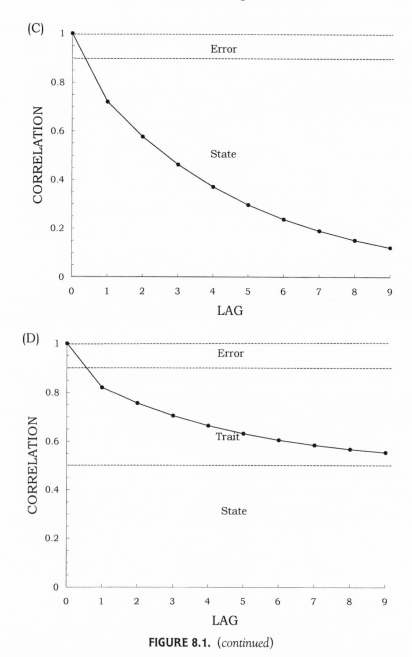

FIGURE 8.1. (*continued*)

ance, we graph the total variance due to that factor. Figure 8.1D clearly shows how the trait–state–error model combines features of the other three models.

This is not to say that the trait–state–error model does not have any weaknesses. As is typical of most very general models, it can be very difficult to estimate. One needs very large sample sizes to estimate the model. Moreover, estimation requires some assumption of *stationarity*—in other words, that the effects due to each factor are the same at each time. Although the trait–state–error model has several important theoretical advantages, it can be difficult to work with empirically. However, we still believe that it does present new possibilities for the analysis and conceptualization of over-time data.

Although we favor stochastic models of change, others have advocated deterministic models in which change is entirely predicted by time of measurement (e.g., McArdle & Epstein, 1987). These models, sometimes called *growth-curve models*, imply that each individual is on a track or orbit. The person may vary about that orbit, but he or she tends to stay near it. An example of a simple deterministic model is that all individuals change in a linear fashion. Some growth-curve models create a pseudosimplex (but not a quasi-simplex) structure of correlations (Rogosa & Willett, 1985). Growth-curve modelers have criticized autoregressive models because such models discard the overall means, whereas growth-curve models leave the mean in the data. Growth-curve models are more parsimonious than the autoregressive model in that growth-curve models explain overall or mean change as well as within-person change. We remain skeptical that maturation is the only plausible explanation of group change. History, instrumentation, mortality, and especially regression toward the mean may be just as plausible explanations. So we worry that it may be very misleading to base one's model on the overall pattern of mean change.

Trait–State–Error Model of Physical Attractiveness

In this example, we illustrate the estimation of the trait–state–error model (Kenny & Zautra, 1995). The model is an extension of the autoregressive model, but it allows for a trait or unchanging factor. The example concerns regression toward the mean of physical attractiveness across the lifespan.

In this section, we reanalyze the data previously analyzed by Zebrowitz, Olson, and Hoffman (1993), who examined physical attractiveness measured at five times during the lifespan. Our conclusions are very similar to those of Zebrowitz et al. (1993) despite some differences in our analyses. Their data consist of three childhood measures (average age 10), three puberty measures (average age 14.5 for males and age 12.5 for females), three adolescent measures (average age 17.5), one young adult measure (age 31), and one late adult measure (age 56). The measures were for 103 males and 104 females (see Zebrowitz et al., 1993, for a discussion of missing data).

For the model that we estimate, there are three sources of variation:

> *Trait*—lifetime physical attractiveness
> *State*—changes in physical attractiveness
> *Error*—random change

So, if we say, "Joe has always been a good-looking guy," we are referring to the trait component. If we say, "Joe used to be good looking when he was younger, but he no longer is quite so good looking," we are referring to the state component. Finally, if we say, "Joe was a good-looking child," we are referring to the error component. Note that error in this context does not mean error of measurement but rather transient sources of variance, such as "having a bad hair day." However, part of error variance would be errors of measurement.

We estimated a model that is very similar to that estimated by Zebrowitz et al. (1993). A diagram of the model for the state component is given in Figure 8.2. The model is estimated by the structural equation modeling computer program LISREL 8. We treated the first three measures as an indicator of a child factor, the next three as indicators of a puberty factor, the next three as indicators of an adolescence factor, the next measure as an indicator of a young adult factor, and the last measure as an indicator of a late adult factor. When there was more than one indicator, the loadings were set equal. We also forced the error variance of the two single-indicator measures to be equal.

We estimated separate models for males and females. For the model that we present, the fit is excellent. For males the Tucker–Lewis index is .98, and for females the index is 1.00. Because a Tucker–Lewis value of .95 or larger is generally considered a good fit and a fit of 1.00 is optimal, the fit of these models is excellent.

The first major result is that there is little evidence of a trait

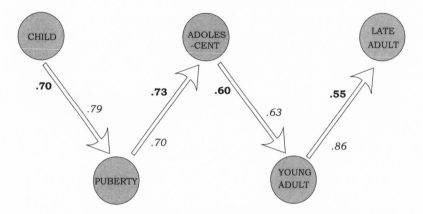

FIGURE 8.2. Estimates of standardized stability in physical attractiveness for males and females across the lifespan: boldface numbers, males; italic numbers, females.

factor. For neither males nor females is there any evidence of statistically significant trait variance. Dropping the trait factor did not statistically significantly reduce the fit for males $[\chi^2(1) = 1.06]$ and for females $[\chi^2(1) = 1.62]$. Thus, physical attractiveness is not an inherent characteristic of the person. Individuals' attractiveness seems to regress to one population mean.

Figure 8.2 presents the second major result, which is that the rate of change is greater when people are younger. The numbers in boldface are for males and those in italic are for females. For instance, for females the year-to-year correlation in physical attractiveness when they are young is .94, whereas during the last interval the year-to-year correlation is .99. For males, the year-to-year correlation is .91 when they are young and .98 when they are old. Across the entire lifespan there is considerable change: the correlation from age 10 to age 56 is .26 for females and .19 for males. These translate into year-to-year changes of .97 for females and .96 for males. We can see why we find no trait variance for physical attractiveness. High year-to-year stabilities translate into very low stability across the lifespan.

In the last set of models, we modeled the rate of change from year to year. We transformed years to a logarithmic scale and assumed that the rate of change is constant in this metric. So, for instance, we are assuming that the rate of change in physical attractiveness is the same from 10 to 15 years of age as from 30 to 45 (i.e., $10/15 = 30/45 = 2/3$). The fit of this model was quite good for both men and women. Within this model the test–retest correlation from age 10–20 is .53 for females and .52 for males, whereas the test–retest correlation in physical attractiveness during the 50's is .85 for females and .84 for males. Quite clearly the data indicate slower rates of change for older persons than for younger ones.[2]

This example shows an unexpected benefit of regression toward the mean. If you are not especially attractive physically and so become envious of someone else's attractiveness, if you wait long enough, the two of you will not be all that different in physical attractiveness. You may, however, have to wait for 50 years. So, in the long run, men can expect to be as attractive as Mel Gibson (the good news) and Mel Brooks (the bad news). Because regression toward the mean works backward in time, people who are more attractive than you when you are in your 60's were probably only little more attractive than you when you were both 10 years old. Regression toward the mean is the great equalizer.

To most readers, the absence of trait variance in physical attractiveness seems counterintuitive. However, consider the fact that famous child stars often do not grow up to be particularly attractive adults.

Despite our failure to find evidence of trait variance in judgments of physical attractiveness, we believe that the trait–state–error model is useful. It allows for careful documentation of different sources of variance.

REGRESSION ARTIFACTS IN MULTIWAVE STUDIES

In Chapters 3, 4, and 5, we discussed how regression toward the mean could create apparent change due to an intervention that is really just a statistical artifact. Those chapters focused on changes with just two waves of measurement. In this section we extend the discussion to the case in which there are more than two waves of measurement. We begin with a graphical analysis and then present

---

[2]A log scale for the exponent in the autoregressive presents an interpretive problem for newborns. Because the log of 0 is $-\infty$, the predicted correlation of physical attractiveness at birth with any time later in life (even the next day) is 0.

a mathematical formulation. We finish with an extended example of a well-known evaluation.

Graphical Analysis

Nesselroade, Stigler, and Baltes (1980) have previously discussed this issue. They have argued that regression toward the mean is more of a problem in two-wave studies and may be less of a problem in multiwave studies. Gottman and Rushe (1993) have reiterated these claims. Lund (1989a, 1989b), while disagreeing with Nesselroade et al. (1980) in some ways, has expressed similar concerns.

Although there is *theoretical* merit in their claims, we strongly differ with these scholars. We believe that the empirical fact of proximal autocorrelation implies that regression toward the mean continues after the second wave of measurement. We worry that the careful qualifications made by the aforementioned scholars might be lost on the novice. We hope that this primer has made it abundantly clear that regression toward the mean is a serious problem.

Our disagreement centers on the assumption of proximal auto-correlation. As Nesselroade et al. (1980) make clear, if that assumption were false, regression toward the mean would be less of a problem. We, however, are confident that proximal autocorrelation is the rule, not the exception. We urge an extensive look at the myriad of over-time correlation matrices to measure the degree of proximal autocorrelation.

Nesselroade et al. (1980) are correct in stating that the largest amount of regression toward the mean usually takes place at lag 1 (r_{12} vs. r_{13} or r_{14}) because that is where the correlation changes most. To see this, the reader should examine the changes in correlation over time in Figure 8.1 and see that the largest decline is at lag 1. However, regression toward the mean continues in further waves. One case that Nesselroade et al. (1980) considered is a pure trait model (see Table 8.2A or Figure 8.1A). For that model, all of the regression toward the mean occurs at lag one. However, we believe that such correlational structures are rarely encountered empirically, a view that underlies the distrust of repeated measures analysis of variance for such data.

Figure 8.3 is intended to expand the usual two-wave illustration of the regression artifact due to matching, but with the normal distributions of measures for the two groups turned on their sides. Figure 8.3 attempts to extend the regression artifact from matching

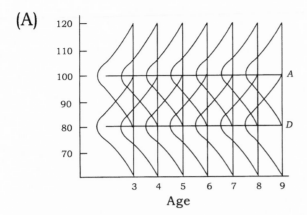

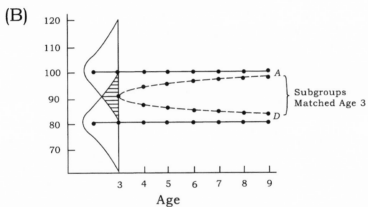

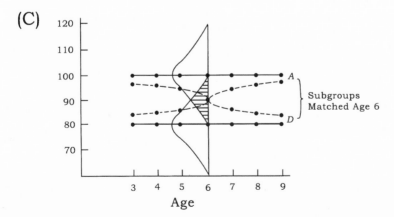

FIGURE 8.3. Mean trends in two groups (mean difference of 20 points) as a function of matching at age 3 or 6 years. Adapted from Campbell (1996). Copyright 1996 by Pergamon Press. Adapted by permission of Elsevier Science.

on a single year to more years—earlier as well as subsequent years. We assume that there are seven waves of data for two neighborhoods of children from ages 3–9. Within each group, we have assumed a first-order autoregressive model. (The correlational structure is similar to that of Table 8.2, part C.) We have separated the two groups by 2 within-group standard deviations.

In Figure 8.3A, the group means for two neighborhoods, A (advantaged) and D (disadvantaged), on an annual vocabulary test are normed so as to remove the differential growth that would accompany different means for an absolute measure such as total vocabulary. The advantaged neighborhood has a mean of 100; the disadvantaged, a mean of 80. We have set the standard deviation within each group at 10. The two neighborhoods show the same overlap in each year as shown by the normal distribution curves.

In Figure 8.3B, the expected values are portrayed in subsequent (and earlier) years for subgroups matched on the age 3 measure at the score of 90. The separation of the age 3 matches grows larger as the number of years separating the two measures increases, in conformity with the lower correlation coefficients. Consistent with Nesselroade et al. (1980), the largest amount of regression occurs between the ages of 3 and 4. However regression continues, even between years 8 and 9.

In Figure 8.3C, the effects of a hypothetical matching of scores at age 6 are shown. Note especially that there is regression toward earlier means as well as toward later ones. Regression toward the mean occurs in both directions, a fact that we exploit in Chapter 10.

One might have used the years 3–6 as the matching base; that is, one might match at age 6 using the average of years 3–6 as the matching variable. If this were done, matching, as well as statistical equating, would never reduce the difference between neighborhoods in any one year to 0. Due to the proximally autocorrelated correlational structure, the difference would be smallest for ages 4 and 5, doing less well at ages 3 and 6. Most importantly, the gap between neighborhoods would widen from ages 7–9. Thus, matching on or "controlling" for 4 years of data does not eliminate pseudoeffects.

Multiple regression adjustments still predominate in the quasi-experimental compensatory education literature, and the proximately autocorrelated nature of the data generates not only pseudoeffects but also pseudotrends of decreasing (or increasing) effects in long-term follow-up (Director, 1979). Thus, regression artifacts could create pseudoeffects that are not really present in the data.

Measurement of Trend Differences

Consider two groups, a treatment group and a control group. The mean of the treatment group is denoted as M_T, and the mean of the control group as M_C. We assume stationarity, and so the mean and the variances do not change over time. If we were to match control and treatment participants at one time, these scores would regress to different means and so there would be a gap. As presented in Table 2.1 in Chapter 2, the amount of regression of the predicted score for X_2 given X_1 equals $r_{12}(X_1 - M) + M$ when the mean and variance do not change over time and where r_{12} is the correlation between X_1 and X_2. As we discuss in Chapter 5, when we use this formula in both groups, the predicted separation between groups is

$$(M_T - M_C)(1 - r)$$

where $M_T - M_C$ is the difference between groups at the time of matching, and r is the pooled correlation within groups between waves. Given that the separation in group means depends on the correlation and given a proximally autocorrelated structure, the gap between treatment groups widens as the distance from the point of matching increases. We can see the widening gap in Figure 8.3B and 8.3C. An empirical example of a pseudo-widening gap is presented in the next section.

The trait–state–error model can be used to better understand issues that were raised in Chapter 5 about the size of the gap between treatment groups. One explanation for why there is a gap between groups at the pretest is that the groups differ on the trait, state, and error factors. Thus, change in the error and the state factors should reduce the gap. If, however, selection into groups is not based on the error variance, then there should be less regression toward the mean and the slope (b_{21}) must be corrected for attenuation, that is, divided by its reliability. Finally, if selection is based entirely on the trait factor, then we would expect that there would be no narrowing of the gap and some sort of change score analysis would be appropriate though assumptions of stationarity would be required. In general, if we are to successfully correct for pretest differences in selection, we must know what factors (trait, state, and error) created that pretest difference. However, it can be difficult to know exactly what the sources of selection are. This is the fundamental problem in the analysis of multiwave quasi-experimental studies.

Before turning to the example, we briefly consider the paper by Gibbons, Hedeker, and Davis (1987), who artfully illustrate that regression toward the mean can create a pseudocovariation between two curves over time. They were interested in the association between two trend lines. The title of their paper is "Regression toward the Mean: More on the Price of Beer and the Salaries of Priests." Their thesis is straightforward. If there is selection on a variable, then over time that variable regresses to its mean. So two different variables are selected, they both regress to their means, and the two trends then mirror one another. But that covariation of trends is an artifact due to regression toward the mean.

A Job-Training Example

In this subsection, we consider the divergence of trend lines in an actual quasi-experimental evaluation. The next two figures come from a famous study of a job-training program by Ashenfelter (1978). As graphed (Campbell, 1975, 1996; Cook & Campbell, 1979, Figure 5.9, p. 229), this is the most effective intervention of which we know. Most job-training studies show either no benefits or pseudoharmful ones (Director, 1979). Ashenfelter (1978) used records from 10 years of earnings subject to withholding tax for individuals receiving job training in 1963/64, and for age, gender, and race matches not receiving such training. We consider here only the data of white males, although essentially the same points can be made for African-American males.

From Figures 8.4, we see that there are sustained differences between the groups during 1959–1963 even before the intervention begins. Using the vocabulary from Chapter 5, we observe that the program is a compensatory program in that the treated group's income is lower than the control group's before the intervention. After the intervention, there is a dramatic catch-up from 1965 to 1969. We note visually (implicitly using raw change analysis) that it looks as though the treatment effects are sustained to an undiminished degree.

Ashenfelter (1978) did not present the graph in Figure 8.4, but instead he adjusted values in which the yearly data for 1963–1969 were "corrected" or "statistically equated" by use of the pooled data from the years 1959–1962 as covariates. In Figure 8.5, we present his effect estimates, again for white males. Because the covariate is based upon four pooled years, the correlation with a subsequent year is very high and the adjustment initially almost entirely removes the difference between treatment group means. But during the later years, the multiple correlation between 1959–1962

FIGURE 8.4. Trend lines for white males in the treatment and control groups (a replotting of results from Ashenfelter, 1978). Adapted from Campbell (1996). Copyright 1996 by Pergamon Press. Adapted by permission of Elsevier Science.

and the target year undoubtedly becomes lower and lower due to the proximally autocorrelated nature of such data. The adjustment thus becomes less and less, showing in Ashenfelter's statistics as steadily *declining* benefits. In Figure 8.5, we have graphed his estimates of gains using statistical equating in contrast with the visual impression (i.e., using change scores). Figure 8.5 clearly shows that with statistical equating the effect entirely disappears. However, a visual inspection or raw change scores analysis clearly shows that after training the gap narrows and the program is beneficial.

We are somewhat ambivalent about this illustration, for we believe that in most cases the impact of many interventions does steadily diminish (Campbell, 1988, pp. 308–312), in compatibility with Ashenfelter's (1978) reported results. But, equally strongly, we believe that Ashenfelter's method would have produced diminishing results even if the interventions' impact had, in truth, been undiminished.

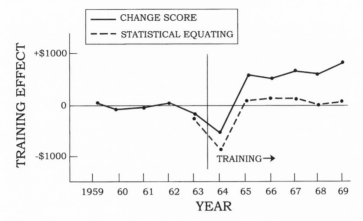

FIGURE 8.5. Treatment effect estimates of job training for white males using statistical equating and change score analysis (Ashenfelter, 1978). Adapted from Campbell (1996). Copyright 1996 by Pergamon Press. Adapted by permission of Elsevier Science.

Figure 8.6 is reproduced from an unpublished presentation by Campbell and Reichardt (1983), and for that presentation Reichardt conducted a simulation of what would have happened if in an Ashenfelter-like situation there had been no measurable effect. Reichardt generated a first-order autoregressive model in which

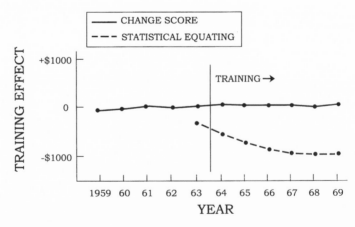

FIGURE 8.6. Simulation by Campbell and Reichardt (1983) of a no-effect model using statistical equating and change score analysis. Adapted from Campbell (1996). Copyright 1996 by Pergamon Press. Adapted by permission of Elsevier Science.

there is a constant $1,000 difference between treatment groups, the treated respondents earning less income than the controls. For this model, statistical equating would have made the job-training program look increasingly harmful! Of course, we do not know whether the model that was generated for Ashenfelter's data is indeed the correct model of selection. But if the two groups are drawn from different populations (i.e., selection on a trait), then his analysis is very misleading.

CONCLUSION

If we are to understand regression artifacts in longitudinal research, we need to first understand the correlational structure over time. A pure trait model is usually insufficient to explain the correlational structure because data are typically proximally autocorrelated: adjacent waves of data are more highly correlated than nonadjacent waves. First-order autoregressive models can explain this structure. In this model, scores are assumed to be caused by the prior wave of measurement. The trait–state–error model combines the trait model with the autoregressive model.

Regression artifacts are a subtle source of mistaken causal inferences from longitudinal studies. Not only are these regression artifacts produced by matching cases on fallible pretests or other measures, but they also occur in analyses that anchor statistical adjustments of outcome variables on "independent" variables taken at a specific time. The anchoring measures (just like the matching variables) are implicitly treated as though they were perfect, lacking measurement error and reliable irrelevant variance.

In longitudinal studies with many periodic waves of measurement, anchoring the analysis (as by matching or statistical equating) at any one time period (usually the first wave) is likely to produce an ever-increasing pseudoeffect as the time interval increases. The degree to which the resulting differential trends are merely regression artifacts can be estimated, and thus we can attempt to distinguish them from genuine effects.

A key question is whether persons are regressing to the same mean or persons or subsets of persons are regressing to different means. One can answer this question by estimating the trait–state–error model. If there is variance due to trait, then individuals are regressing toward their own different means. If there is not trait variance, then all individuals are regressing to the same mean. For details concerning the estimation of such models, consult Kenny and Zautra (1995).

We need to emphasize the conclusions drawn from multiwave studies may depend on the model that is being assumed. Although we prefer trait–state–error models, there are other models (e.g., growth-curve models and second-order autoregressive models). Very often empirical analysis is unable to select among these models. The researcher should consider what type of model is most sensible for the particular application.

We have nearly completed our discussion of regression artifacts. Next, in the penultimate chapter, we consider further the issue of proximal autocorrelation in the case in which two variables are changing over time. It is an implicit assumption of a neglected statistical method: cross-lagged panel correlation.

9

Cross-Lagged Panel Correlation Analysis

In the previous chapters, we have generally had one variable, a treatment variable that is unchanging and is presumed to cause another variable that is moving through time. Very often the situation is quite different. Two variables are both moving through time and each may cause the other. For historical reasons, we focus on one statistical technique, discussed below. However, our overarching purpose is to encourage researchers to consider alternative models when they analyze longitudinal data.

WHAT IS CLPC ANALYSIS?

This chapter focuses on an analysis technique that one of the present authors invented (Campbell, 1963; Campbell & Stanley, 1963; Rozelle & Campbell, 1969) and the other spent most of his early career developing (Kenny, 1973, 1975b, 1979; Kenny & Harackiewicz, 1979). The technique is called *cross-lagged panel correlation* (commonly abbreviated CLPC, an acronym that we use in this primer). In this chapter, we review the long and contentious literature concerning this technique. We begin with a description of classical CLPC analysis. We show how the method's fundamental logic is based on regression toward the mean and proximal autocorrelation. We then consider criticisms made by David R. Rogosa and others of the method. Next, we consider a recent recasting of CLPC as a variant of multitrait–multimethod matrix analysis. Finally, we provide a series of recommendations for analysis. Although we have defended CLPC in the past (Kenny & Campbell, 1984, 1989), this chapter presents the most detailed defense to date.

The original use of the technique involves two variables. Although the use of cross-lagged correlations for causal inference is nearly 100 years old (Hooker, 1901), the technique grew out of the first author's attempt to generalize Lazarsfeld's (1972) 16-fold table to continuous variables. Two variables, X and Y, are measured at two times, 1 and 2. (Note that X and Y are two different variables and not pretest and posttest, as they were in earlier chapters.) Figure 9.1 illustrates the set of six correlations between the four variables: two synchronous or cross-sectional correlations, two autocorrelations, and two cross-variable and time-lagged or cross-lagged correlations. The essence of traditional CLPC is that if X causes Y more than Y causes X, then $r_{X_1Y_2}$ should be larger than $r_{X_2Y_1}$. If, however, Y causes X more than X causes Y, then $r_{X_2Y_1}$ should be larger than $r_{X_1Y_2}$. Thus, the preponderance of causation is presumed to be measured through a comparison of cross-lagged correlations. However, as we discuss below, causal inference is much more complicated than a simple comparison of two correlations.

As one example of CLPC, Calsyn and Kenny (1977) examined the relative influence of grades on academic self-esteem. The research evidence that was reviewed consistently pointed to the result that grades caused academic self-esteem more than vice versa.

In another analysis, Lefkowitz, Eron, Walder, and Huesmann (1972), as part of the 1972 U.S. Surgeon General's report on the effects of violence on television, studied TV violence and aggressive behavior of 211 boys aged 3 and 13. The 10-year lag makes it one of

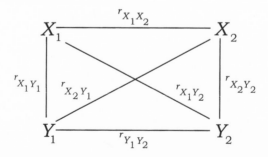

FIGURE 9.1. CLPC paradigm of six possible correlations.

the longest ever studied using CLPC. These authors concluded that TV violence had a greater causal effect on aggressive behavior than vice versa.

To test whether the difference between the two cross-lagged correlations is statistically significant, one should not use a Fisher's z test because the correlations are themselves correlated. Two tests of the differences between cross-lagged correlations are currently available: one is the Pearson–Filon test as modified by Steiger (1980), and the other is a test recently developed by Raghunathan, Rosenthal, and Rubin (1996).

As initially suggested by Rozelle and Campbell (1969) and as elaborated by Kenny (1973, 1975b, 1979; see also Duncan, 1972), CLPC is a test of spuriousness. The view is that the correlation between variables does not reflect the mutual causation between the two but is due to a common variable that causes them both. In experimental research, researchers typically take as the null hypothesis that there is no causal relationship between the two variables and so any association between the two variables is viewed as evidence of a causal effect of the experimental variable on the outcome. In nonexperimental research, it is likely that there is a correlation between the variables even in the presence of no direct causal relation. If we assume, akin to the null hypothesis in experimental research, no direct causal effects between the variables in the model, then the source of that covariation between the variables is most plausibly viewed as spurious. One or more variables external to the variables under consideration can bring about that correlation.

One plausible model of spuriousness is presented in Figure 9.2. The variable Z brings about the correlations between the two variables X and Y. We follow the usual convention of circling latent variables. Within this model of spuriousness, the effect of the spurious variable on both X and Y does not change over time ($a_1 = a_2$ and $b_1 = b_2$). This assumption of the stationarity of effects has two important consequences: equal synchronous correlations and equal cross-lagged correlations. So the equal synchronous correlations can be used to test the stationarity assumption, and the equal cross-lagged correlations can be used to test the assumption of spuriousness. We consider later in this chapter the very strong assumption of stationarity.

In Chapter 8, we discussed the concept of proximal autocorrelation: the same construct measured close together in time correlates more strongly than when measured farther apart in time. The

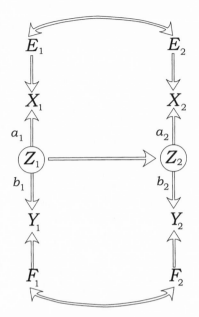

FIGURE 9.2. CLPC model of spuriousness.

CLPC model of spuriousness is based on this principle but in a bivariate sense: a pair of variables measured at the same time should correlate more strongly than the same pair measured at different times (see also Chapters 6 and 7). To simplify presentation, the variable X is a dichotomy whose two values are denoted as A and B. We assume that X is changing over time but that the proportions of A's and B's are the same at both times. We also assume that the variance of Y is the same at both times. Given these assumptions, it can be shown that the correlation between X (dummy coded) and Y is directly proportional to the mean difference on Y between the A's and the B's. We focus on this mean difference.

We present the mean differences in the A's and B's in Figure 9.3, a variant of a Galton squeeze diagram. We have graphed the means on Y_1 and Y_2 for the two levels of X_1, M_A and M_B. The upper lines in the figure refer to M_A values, and the bottom lines to the M_B values. As in a Galton squeeze diagram, we have connected the means from the same persons.

Consider first the solid lines, which refer to the A's and B's on X at time 1 or M_{A_1} and M_{B_1}). At time 1, there is a larger separation in the means than there is at time 2, the principle of proximal auto-

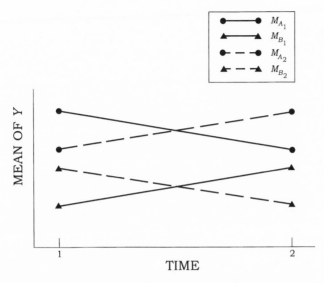

FIGURE 9.3. Illustration of regression toward the mean in both temporal directions for a bivariate relation.

correlation. Over time, both means regress to the same mean and so the gap between the means narrows from time 1 to time 2: there is regression toward the mean. The gap at time 1 is directly related to $r_{X_1Y_1}$, and the gap at time 2 is related to $r_{X_1Y_1}$. Thus, this regression toward the mean implies that $r_{X_1Y_1}$ is larger than $r_{X_1Y_2}$.

Also in Figure 9.3, we consider the A's and B's on X at time 2. We have plotted the means for Y_2 and Y_1 for the two groups (M_{A_2} and M_{B_2}). Note that because the variable X is changing, some of the A's at time 2 were B's at time 1 and vice versa. We have connected the means using dashed lines. Again we see regression toward the mean, but now that regression toward the mean is backward in time, which implies that $r_{X_2Y_2}$ is larger than $r_{X_2Y_1}$. Note in Figure 9.3 that the size of the gaps between the two Y means is the same when we look at synchronous correlations (the larger gaps in means) and the cross-lagged relationships (the smaller gaps). CLPC rests on the assumption of proximal autocorrelation. Given stationarity, the degree of regression toward the mean ought to be the same regardless of the temporal direction. If X does not cause Y or vice versa, equal cross-lagged correlations would be implied by regression toward the mean and stationarity.

COMPLICATIONS IN CLPC ANALYSIS

In traditional CLPC analysis, a comparison of cross-lagged correlations points to which variable causes the other. The simple bivariate comparison of correlations is complicated by three problems: direction of causation, shifts in communality, and a model of causality. These three topics are considered in the following subsections.

Direction of Causation

Following Yee and Gage (1968) and Rozelle and Campbell (1969), we note that there is a complication concerning the inference of the direction of causation within CLPC. Imagine that $r_{X_1Y_2}$ is greater than $r_{X_2Y_1}$. Traditional CLPC would conclude that X causes increases in Y. The alternative hypothesis is that Y causes decreases in X. Both explanations are possible. One way to determine the relative plausibility of the two alternatives is to examine the synchronous correlations. If those correlations are positive, then it seems more plausible that X causes increases in Y. If negative, then it is more plausible that Y causes decreases in X. If the synchronous correlations were near 0, then theory or the absolute size of the cross-lagged correlations would suggest the direction of causation.

Shifts in Communality

A decrease in the reliability of X or an increase in the reliability of Y might plausibly explain why the cross-lagged correlations might differ. Recall that a key assumption of CLPC is stationarity: the effect of the spurious variable on the measures is the same at time 1 and time 2. Using Figure 9.2, the assumption is made that $a_1 = a_2$ and $b_1 = b_2$. It seems doubtful that such an equality constraint would hold, especially with standardized variables (Cudeck, 1989).

CLPC researchers recognized these difficulties. Beginning with Crano, Kenny, and Campbell (1972), corrections for changes in communality have been made to the cross-lagged correlations. Communality represents variance in the measure that is shared with other measures. The measure of change in communality within CLPC is the ratio of time 2 communality of a variable divided by the time 1 communality of that same variable, something called a *communality ratio*.

A method developed by the second author looks at changes in the synchronous correlations and then adjusts the cross-lagged correlations for changes in communality. Moreover, tests can be done to determine if the communality shifts can be used to explain the changes in the synchronous correlations over time. Relatively simple approaches to the estimation of communality ratios are given in Kenny (1979), and more formal methods are given in Kenny and Harackiewicz (1979). Later in this chapter, we present the approach of Kenny and Campbell (1989) to correction for shifts in communality.

We need to be clear about exactly what stationarity assumptions are made with these corrections. The stationarity assumption is still made, but it does not necessarily refer to the standardized or unstandardized metric. Rather, it states that effects are stationary over time in some metric which is a linear transformation of the original (or standardized) metric.

A Causal Model of CLPC

If the cross-lagged correlations are unequal, what does that imply about causality? The only CLPC paper that explicitly examined a model of causality is that of Kenny (1973). In that paper, a cross-lagged common factor is introduced. It is assumed that one variable, say X, is caused by that factor and that the other variable, say Y, is caused by that same factor but with a lag. Given such a model, we would not conclude so firmly that X caused Y, but rather that X is a leading indicator and that Y is a lagging indicator. The model developed by Kenny (1973) for CLPC is not really a model of causation per se, at least not in the usual way that causality is discussed. For example, lightening precedes thunder, but we would not say that lightening *causes* thunder. Rather, it shows only that the speed of light is faster than the speed of sound.

CLPC does not have a very rich model of causation. Unequal cross-lagged correlations show only that one variable leads the other. Even that conclusion may be mistaken if the leading variable may, in reality, be a lagging variable that loads negatively on the cross-lagged common factor (see the earlier discussion of direction of causation). Finally, we do not measure the bidirectional strength of causation.[1]

---

[1]Rozelle and Campbell (1969) did suggest a "no cause baseline," but Kenny (1973) showed that the logic of their procedure was faulty.

THE ROGOSA CRITIQUE

In a pair of widely cited papers, Rogosa (1979, 1980) criticized the use of CLPC. Others had previously criticized the method (Bohrnstedt, 1969; Duncan, 1969), and so many of Rogosa's criticisms were made before. Rogosa's (1980) conclusion is remarkably blunt: "CLC [cross-lagged panel correlation] is best forgotten" (p. 257). He appears to have gotten his wish, because his papers, especially the 1980 *Psychological Bulletin* paper, led to a precipitous decline in the publication of studies that used the method. Even Cook and Campbell (1979) favorably cited the analysis of Rogosa. Today, we see only an occasional reference to CLPC (Mullen & Cooper, 1994; Rosenthal & Rosnow, 1991).

The model that Rogosa and other critics have assumed is quite different from the model in Figure 9.2. He used as his fundamental model of causal effects the model that we present in Figure 9.4. In this model, X and Y directly cause each other with a time lag. (In this chapter, when we say "causal effects," we usually mean the effect from X_1 to Y_2 and the effect from Y_1 to X_2. Technically, effects from spurious variables are causal, but we typically are not referring to those effects when we use the term "causal.") The two variables may be correlated at time 1, and that correlation is represented by a curved line between X_1 and Y_1. The correlation between X_2 and Y_2 may be larger than can be explained by the causation between variables, and so there is a correlation between the unexplained variation in X_2 and Y_2, the curved line between U and V. The model in Figure 9.4 can be directly estimated by multiple regression. The time-1 variables are treated as predictor variables, and each of the time-2 variables is treated as an outcome variable. The correlation

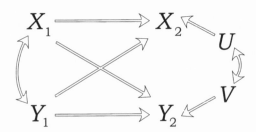

FIGURE 9.4. Two-variable, two-time model of causal effects assumed by Rogosa (1980): the multiple regression model. Adapted from Rogosa (1980). Copyright 1980 by the American Psychological Association. Adapted by permission.

between U and V can be estimated by the partial correlation between X_2 and Y_2, controlling for X_1 and Y_1. The regression coefficients, either standardized or unstandardized, provide estimates of the causal paths. Given this fact about estimation, we shall refer to the model in Figure 9.4 as the *multiple regression model*.

The multiple regression model does not imply equal cross-lagged correlations. As Rogosa (1980) has shown, given zero cross-causal paths, the cross-lagged correlations are equal to each other only when the stability paths (the paths from X_1 to X_2 and from Y_1 to Y_2) are equal. Because such equal stabilities are unlikely, equal cross-lagged correlations provide a poor way to diagnose no causal effects, if one takes the model in Figure 9.4 as the representation of reality.

The major difficulty with the multiple regression model is how it explains spuriousness: at time 1, it posits covariation between X and Y without really modeling that covariation; at time 2, covariation magically reappears. Curved lines in path diagrams of structural models imply covariation, but the model does not explain the causal process that explains the source of that covariation.

Dwyer (1986) has determined that the multiple regression model implicitly makes what would seem to be a very implausible assumption about spuriousness. Figure 9.5 contains his model. He begins with the basic multiple regression model of Rogosa and no

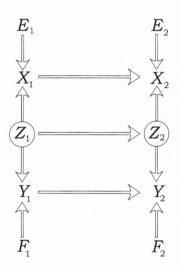

FIGURE 9.5. Dwyer's (1986) elaboration of the multiple regression model for spuriousness.

causation (see Figure 9.4): X_1 causes X_2 and Y_1 causes X_2, and no cross-causal effects. Like the CLPC model in Figure 9.2, Z acts as the spurious cause of X and Y. Thus, unlike the regression model, we have a model of spuriousness. We can now ask, as Dwyer (1966) did, the following question: given the model in Figure 9.5, when will multiple regression yield estimates of "causal" paths of 0? The answer is that multiple regression will yield such estimates when Z is totally unstable over time (i.e., when the path from Z_1 to Z_2 is 0). It seems extraordinarily unlikely that the spurious factor has zero stability. Thus, the multiple regression model makes a very implausible assumption about the nature of the spurious factor and does not really allow for meaningful spurious factors.

In Chapter 8, we developed the trait–state–error model. That is, a variable is conceived as having three fundamental components: a *trait* (or unchanging) component, a *state* (or slowly changing) component, and an *error* (or totally unstable) component. The multiple regression model in Figure 9.4 implicitly presumes that both X and Y are entirely state variables. If there is any error or trait variance, the model is incorrect and the causal paths may be biased. We now consider the effect of these possible specification errors on the estimates of the causal effects.

We first consider the presence of measurement error, a topic that we previously considered in Chapter 5. The presence of error variance is complicated because both X and Y are likely to be measured with error. The presence of measurement error in X_1 tends to lower the estimate of its effects on X_2 and Y_2, but the measurement error in Y_1 likely tends to raise the estimate of the effect of X_1 on those variables. (We are assuming that all correlations and paths are positive.) When the reliabilities of X_1 and Y_1 are comparable, these two biases tend approximately to cancel each other out, but there is no absolute guarantee. Although it can be difficult to determine whether measurement error results in over- or underestimation of causal effects, it is usually the case that measurement error biases estimates of effects. Currently, the most common way of controlling for these biasing effects is to measure variables with multiple indicators and perform a latent variable analysis.[2] (True-score estimation is currently not a workable strategy when there are two causal variables that are unreliable.) Structural equation modeling programs (such as AMOS, CALIS, EQS, or LISREL) can be used to estimate effects within latent-variable causal models.

---

[2]Because of correlated measurement across the same measure at different times, at least three indicators per construct are necessary for this model to be identified. However, if the constructs are correlated, two indicators are sufficient.

The presence of trait variance also generally leads to bias in the estimation of causal effects. There has, however, been very little previous investigation of the biasing effects of trait variance on causal effects, although the work of Heise (1970) is a notable exception. It is much more complicated to describe the effect of trait variance on the regression coefficients than it is to describe the effect of measurement error. We begin by assuming that the effects of trait and state do not change over time and that there are no cross-causal effects. If the proportion of trait variance is larger for X than for Y, then, other things being equal, X's effect on Y is overestimated and Y's effect on X is underestimated. Even if the amount of trait variance is equal for both X and Y, the strength of the synchronous correlations must be the same for the trait and state factors for the estimates of causal impacts to be unbiased. The presence of trait variance greatly complicates the estimates of causal effects using multiple regression. The combined effects of differential trait variance in the measures, differential correlation between trait and state factors across variables, and differential stabilities of the two state factors all make the multiple regression estimates quite misleading. Interesting, CLPC need only assume that the state stabilities for the two measures are equal; no assumption needs to be made about the equality of the proportions of variance or the relative degree of correlation between traits and states. Further study of the biasing effects of trait variance on multiple regression estimates is urgently needed.

If we accept the model in Figure 9.4, the major advantage of the multiple regression model is that it directly measures the causal effects from X to Y and from Y to X. Unlike CLPC, it measures the absolute causal effects in both directions. With CLPC, at best one obtains a measure of relative causality. The major weakness of the multiple regression model is that it does not have a plausible explanation of spuriousness in that if there is a spurious variable, it must be assumed to be totally unstable. A further weakness of the multiple regression model is that corrections must be made for errors of measurement in the predictor variables and strong assumptions must be made about trait variance.

CLPC AS A SPECIAL CASE OF THE MULTITRAIT–MULTIMETHOD MATRIX MODEL

Kenny and Campbell (1989) provided an elaborate formal model for multivariate, two-wave longitudinal data. Like the traditional CLPC model of spuriousness, it presumes that the variables are all caused by a set of unmeasured factors or latent variables. Once corrections are made for shifts in communality or nonstationarity, the effect of the factors on the variables is assumed not to vary over time. Not assumed by traditional CLPC, this model presumes that the standardized stabilities of all the latent variables are the same.

The model that we proposed in 1989 can be estimated by structural equation modeling methods. The stability of the latent variables, assumed to be equal, and the reliabilities of each measure can be estimated. Moreover, the fit of the model can be evaluated, and so it can be determined if the model is inconsistent with the data. In this way a model of spuriousness can be deemed implausible. Of course, a poor-fitting model may indicate a violation of stationarity assumptions, not a violation of spuriousness.

We were not aware of this then, but the model that we presented in 1989 is a variant of multiplicative multitrait–multimethod matrix (MTMM) analysis. Campbell and Fiske (1959) are the inventors of this matrix. The MTMM is a correlation matrix that results when a set of traits is measured by a common set of methods. For longitudinal data, the measures serve as traits and the times serve as the methods. In the more usual additive MTMM analysis, method variance is added to the correlations. So two traits measured by the same method correlate too highly because of shared method variance.

The logic of the multiplicative MTMM model is quite different from the additive model. We start with the true synchronous correlations (or covariances), which are assumed to be the same at all times (i.e., they are stationary). The cross-lagged correlations are smaller than the synchronous correlations, and the ratio of the cross-lagged to the synchronous correlations is a constant; that constant can be interpreted as a stability coefficient. Each variable in the model has its own error variance that may vary across time.

Despite the relative simplicity of the theoretical model, these multiplicative MTMM models are not very easy to estimate. There are phantom variables (nonsubstantive variables) and many parameters whose substantive meaning for most can be difficult to decipher. In Kenny and Campbell (1989), we proposed a new method to estimate these models that is simpler than the usual way that multiplicative MTMM models are estimated (Millsap, 1995). However, our method is itself still fairly complex, and we currently do not know for certain whether the two different methods are exactly equivalent, though we think that they are. Although not straightforward to estimate, we believe multiplicative models are worth all of the difficulties.

We might ask what the implications of the trait–state model (see Chapter 8) are for this MTMM analysis. That analysis implicitly assumes that the ratio of trait variance to state variance is the same for each measure. As discussed above, this is the very same assumption about trait variance that was made for the multiple regression model. The estimate of stability for the MTMM model can be viewed as a weighted average of the stability of the trait factor and the stability of the state factors.

Beginning with Campbell and Fiske (1959), there is a long history of methodologists recommending the MTMM model for analysis of longitudinal data. More recently, there have been suggestions that a multiplicative MTMM is appropriate for the analysis of longitudinal data (Kenny & Campbell, 1989), although see Coleman (1994) for a cautionary note. The model was quite successful at explaining the covariation of the Educational Testing Service Growth Study (Kenny & Campbell, 1989), a data set that has been extensively analyzed. Nonetheless, we know of no practicing researchers who have employed the multiplicative MTMM analysis in estimation of their longitudinal data. We hope to see increased use of MTMM analysis of such data.

CONCLUSION: WHAT IS TO BE DONE?

What is an analyst of longitudinal data to do? We have seen that CLPC has an elaborate model of spuriousness but its model of causation is very limited. The multiple regression approach has an explicit model of causality and the two causal effects can be simultaneously estimated, but its model of spuriousness is quite implausible. So neither model allows for both spuriousness and causality.

The reader might wonder why a combined model of spuriousness and causality cannot be estimated. We are very confident that if such a model were specified, it would not be identified. That is, virtually any data set that could be collected would be consistent with such a model. Moreover, there would not be a unique solution for such a model's parameters. Identification places stringent constraints on the estimation of models, and so a reasonable model that allowed for unspecified spurious factors and causation is most likely impractical. So we find ourselves on the horns of a dilemma: either we can estimate a detailed model of spuriousness but a poor model of causal effects or we can estimate a detailed model of causal effects but a poor model of spuriousness. Perhaps in time a combined model can be estimated, but we remain dubious. Moreover, we have limited ourselves to two waves of data, and having more than two waves may afford some special advantage.

The choice of which model to estimate largely depends on the purposes of the researcher. If the goal is exploratory and the expectation is that there are few, if any, causal effects, then a CLPC analysis is preferable. Should a CLPC analysis be planned, we would recommend the multiplicative MTMM version (Kenny & Campbell, 1989; Millsap, 1995) discussed earlier in this chapter. If, however, there are expected causal effects, then a multiple regression analysis is a reasonable way to estimate causal paths, assuming that some allowance for measurement error in the variables can be made.

We strongly urge that some form of CLPC be used as a screening device before attempting causal analysis. The data analyst needs to show that spuriousness cannot explain the covariation between the variables. We believe that CLPC should be used before causal effects are estimated. The logic of null hypothesis testing in randomized experimental research is first to assume that there are no causal effects and second to look for evidence that is inconsistent with this viewpoint. This is essentially the same perspective as that taken within CLPC. However, most investigators are interested more in showing that covariation between variables is causal than in showing that the covariation is spurious. Previous suggestions that researchers need to first rule out simpler, more parsimonious, noncausal models made earlier by the first author (Brewer, Campbell & Crano, 1970) have largely fallen on deaf ears. We can only repeat the challenge to researchers to rule out the plausible rival hypothesis of spuriousness (i.e., *selection*, using the parlance of Campbell & Stanley, 1963). We return to the necessity of considering plausible rival hypotheses in the concluding chapter of this primer.

So, contrary to what Rogosa asserted in 1980, CLPC is not "best forgotten." Although it is certainly not the causal divining rod that some (including ourselves) once thought that it might be, it should still play a role in the analysis of longitudinal data. We hope that investigators will consider using this method or some other method demonstrating that the association between variables cannot be explained by spuriousness. The mindless use of multiple regression with longitudinal data ought to be overcome.

10

Conclusion

In this chapter, we revisit many of the major themes of the primer: time-reversed analysis, graphical display of results, the importance of design, and consideration of plausible rival hypotheses. Each of these topics is reviewed, but we focus most extensively on time-reversed analysis because it is an excellent way to diagnose a regression artifact. We begin with a brief discussion of epistemology.

In this primer, we have occasionally discussed issues of prediction. In the penultimate section of this chapter we focus on the topic of prediction. We consider how forecasters need to make allowances for regression toward the mean in making predictions. Much of what we discuss in that section is counterintuitive.

This chapter is a bit of a hodgepodge. It contains several disparate topics that we have not discussed in the previous chapters.

COMMON SENSE AND DATA ANALYSIS: A BRIEF EPISTEMOLOGICAL EXEGESIS

Science represents a form of knowing, but locomotion in the amoeba also represents a form of knowing—a quest for knowledge—and it should be recognized that we humans are "cousins to the amoeba" (Campbell, 1974). Knowledge processes help organisms adapt to their environments, but knowledge never comes with absolute certainty. We learn about the world that we inhabit, but we never know it perfectly. As we move through our environment, we sometimes run into predators and do not survive. Even scientific knowledge is fallible and mistaken. Not to recognize errors in our perceptions, scientific knowledge, measuring instruments, and research designs is a recipe for disaster.

Very often explanations of scientific knowledge imply that it is superior to common sense, and science is described as a way of knowing the world that does not rely on naive accounts. However, this perspective on common sense is misleading because scientific knowledge rests on implicit beliefs. Common sense and qualitative knowledge form the very foundation of scientific knowledge, even when that knowledge takes on highly quantitative forms. As one of us (Campbell, 1988) has said:

> After all, man is, in his ordinary way, a very competent knower, and qualitative common sense knowing is not replaced by quantitative knowing. Rather quantitative knowing has to trust and build on the qualitative, including ordinary perception. (p. 388)

Certainly, scientific research can contradict ordinary perception. The most famous achievements of science contradict common sense: physics claims that time is relative, and biology claims that humans are the descendants of apes. Again, we quote from previous work (Campbell, 1988):

> We must not suppose that scientific knowing replaces common sense knowing. Rather, science depends upon common sense even though at best it goes beyond it. Science in the end contradicts some items of common sense, but it only does so by trusting the great bulk of the rest of common sense knowledge. (p. 362)

Initially, it is reasonable to be skeptical of scientific results that contradict common sense. Results that seem incredible should be questioned and doubted. Just because they emanate from a scientific laboratory does not mean that they are inherently valid.

Our careers in social-science methodology have mostly been devoted to developing methods that verify common sense. In large part, this primer illustrates how standard statistical techniques such as multiple regression have falsely made compensatory programs look harmful, a result inconsistent with common sense. Our skepticism, generated by common sense, led us to question these results. The analyses that we have proposed are more consistent with common-sense intuitions. In a young science, results that contradict common sense are often due to improper methodological tools.

Common-sense hypotheses do not require common-sense analysis tools.

The second author's research program over the last 20 years has been an elaboration of the theme that social science should verify hypotheses derived from common sense, especially when research results contradict intuition. Consider the following examples:

> Previous surveys of leadership studies by Stogdill (1948) and Mann (1959) had claimed that leadership is not a stable trait. There was not evidence that some people tend to lead and others tend to follow. However, by using specialized research designs and a statistical model, Kenny and Zaccaro (1983) and Zaccaro, Foti, and Kenny (1991) have shown that a person who is leader in one group tends to be a leader in another group with different members.
>
> Newcomb (1979) had found that liking is not reciprocated: if John likes Mary, Mary does not necessarily like John. However, Kenny and Nasby (1980) found that when individual differences were removed (how much John and Mary liked others on average and how much others on average liked John and Mary), liking was reciprocated.
>
> As reviewed by Swann (1984), the dominant view in social psychology is that people do not accurately perceive others' personalities. However, Levesque and Kenny (1993) and Kenny, Kieffer, Smith, Ceplinski, and Kulo (1996) have shown that when perceivers agree with each other, they accurately know other people's personalities.

In each case, elaborate and complicated statistical analyses validated common-sense beliefs that previous research using naive statistical analyses had indicated were false. What was invalid in those conclusions was not their common sense, but rather the naive statistical methods on which they were based.

Knowledge can progress when science can verify what is already known by common sense. An example more than 2,000 years old, taken from Dunham (1994), illustrates this point. Euclid was ridiculed by his contemporaries for his proof that one side of a triangle is always shorter than the sum of the other two sides. His critics pointed out that even an ass knew this fact, and it was silly to prove the obvious. But by doing so, Euclid and the Greeks laid the foundation for many proofs of theorems that are not so obvious. Moreover, Euclidean geometry laid the foundations for non-

Euclidean geometry, which does indeed show that the shortest distance between two points is not a straight line! Science and mathematics build on common sense and can only contradict some common-sense beliefs by accepting many others.

TIME-REVERSED ANALYSIS[1]

One simple principle that we found of value is to repeat the analysis reversing what physicists have called the *arrow of time*. The purpose of time-reversed analysis (Kenny & Campbell, 1984) is to reanalyze the data to check for regression artifacts. The essence of a time-reversed analysis is a reanalysis of the data in which the temporal ordering of the data is reversed. So, for instance, if in the original analysis all time-2 measures are treated as dependent variables and all time-1 measures as independent variables, the time-reversed analysis would repeat the same analysis but make the time-1 measures the dependent variables and the time-2 measures the independent variables. A time-reversed analysis obeys the biblical declaration that "the first shall be last and the last shall be first."

Imagine the following temporally ordered readings of a physiological variable:

$$53, 56, 59, 52, 55, 57, 75, 76, 73, 71, 78$$

Note that there is a sharp jump from 57 to 75 in the data. This jump from 57 to 75 is also readily apparent when the numbers are reversed in time:

$$78, 71, 73, 76, 75, 57, 55, 52, 59, 56, 53$$

However, instead of the jump in the first series, we now have a decline. In this simple analysis, reversing the flow of time reverses the direction of the effect. This is the fundamental principle of a time-reversed analysis: reversing the temporal ordering of the data and reanalyzing the data should reverse the direction of the effect. If the direction of the effect is not reversed but appears to be "robust," then it is most likely an artifact brought about by regression toward the mean. When both the original and the time-reversed analysis

---

[1]Parts of this section are reprinted from Kenny and Campbell (1984). We thank Lawrence Erlbaum Associates for permission to do so.

yield essentially the same result, then we should lose confidence in the interpretation of the original analysis. Thus, if self-esteem "causes" academic achievement with a causal lag of 1 year, and if a time-reversed analysis—in which prior achievement appears to be "caused" by later self-esteem—yields the same conclusion, then we should view the original conclusion with suspicion.

On the surface, a time-reversed analysis is a nonsensical and downright silly analysis. By itself it does not deserve serious study or attention. But its very "nonsensicalness" provides a logical rationale for the analysis. If the original analysis yields essentially the same results as the nonsensical time-reversed analysis, then perhaps the original analysis is just as nonsensical as the time-reversed analysis.

One parallel to time-reversed analysis is the estimation of equivalent models in structural equation modeling (Kline, 1998). As MacCallum, Wegener, Uchino, and Fabrigar (1993) have pointed out, very often the same model with all the paths backward would fit as well as the original model. A model in which the flow of causality is reversed is in the spirit of time reversal.

There are two prototypical results of a time-reversed analysis. We have just discussed the first prototypical result: essential agreement. For such a result, the time-reversed analysis calls into question the validity of the conclusion of the original analysis. There is one exception. If there is "nothing going on in the data," then both the original and time-reversed analysis should give the same result. When nothing is happening over time, the same result should emerge whether we look forward as the original analysis does or whether we look backward as the time-reversed analysis does.

The second prototypical result is one in which the time-reversed analysis yields results of roughly equal value but opposite sign. In this case, the time-reversed analysis supports the conclusions of the original analysis because looking backward in time produces a "backward" result. If a movie, save a Jim Carey one, is played backward, we know that something is wrong.

To our knowledge, a time-reversed analysis was first employed by Campbell and Clayton (1961). They examined, among other things, the effect of seeing the movie *Gentleman's Agreement* on anti-Semitic attitudes. In the study that they considered, Glock (1951) had examined differences between groups (those who viewed the movie and those who did not) at various levels of initial attitude. Attitudes toward Jews were measured before and after viewing the movie. Campbell and Clayton (1961) suspected that the effect of the motion picture on attitudes in Glock's analysis was, in part, an artifact of regression toward the mean. To demonstrate their point, they argued that "if the apparent effect were only this simple regression [toward the mean], then one should get a similar picture by reversing the temporal arrangement of the table." They performed a time-reversed analysis and found essentially the same result when they reversed the flow of time. Thus, they felt that regression toward the mean explained Glock's results.

Not only were Campbell and Clayton (1961) the first to perform a time-reversed analysis, but they also provided a rationale. They noted that regression toward the mean works both forward and backward in time. Tall parents have shorter children (forward regression), and tall children have shorter parents (backward regression). Thus, if a statistical procedure is biased due to regression toward the mean (i.e., the effect "estimate" is nothing more than regression toward the mean), then a time-reversed analysis should produce an effect estimate with the same sign. If the effect estimate in the original analysis is not due to regression toward the mean, then the effect estimate in the time-reversed analysis should be of the opposite sign. Time-reversed analysis can be viewed as a procedure for rendering regression toward the mean implausible.

A second example of a time-reversed analysis is that of Simonton (1974). In an analysis of archival data, Simonton investigated, among other things, the effects of political instability on creativity through a series of multiple regression analyses. He used the political instability of the prior generation to predict the number of eminent creators in the current generation. Then the regression analysis was repeated, but instead of using the political instability of the *previous* generation, he used the political stability of the *next* generation. He thus predicted backward in time. He found that the "effect" of political instability was much greater when the previous generations were used to predict subsequent events than the reverse.

A third example is taken from Baltes, Nesselroade, Schaie, and Labouvie (1972). They examined the correlation of change with initial status for three cognitive tests. They performed a time-reversed analysis and obtained the same result[2] as that obtained in the original analysis. They concluded that the original results were due to regression toward the mean.

---

[2]Note that because Baltes et al. (1972) did not reverse their change score measure (i.e., posttest minus pretest), they obtained the opposite results. However, had they reversed their measure, they would have obtained the same result.

We introduced the concept of time-reversed analysis into the literature well over 10 years ago, but it is still not yet widely used. The likely reason is that investigators are reluctant to perform statistical analyses that would invalidate their conclusions (see the section below on plausible rival hypotheses).

Certain data analytic procedures have built into them the principles of time-reversed analysis; that is, these procedures guarantee that the time-reversed analysis will have exactly the opposite results from the original analysis. Moreover, these procedures will, when the original analysis shows no effect, also show no effect with a time-reversed analysis.

The simplest of methods that satisfy the time-reversal criteria is McNemar's test of change in a dichotomous measure (see, e.g., Hays, 1963). Given a dichotomy measured at two points of time, the test examines only the "changers." For instance, the shoe manufacturer Nike claims that a greater percentage of persons stick with its brand than any other product. Such a claim is common for a brand that has the largest share of the market. In Table 10.1 we present artificial data that support Nike's claim. At time 2, of the 146 respondents who purchased athletic shoes, Nike held 78% of its consumers while Reebok retained only 69% of its previous consumers. However, a time-reversed analysis yields similar results: Nike "retained" 82% and Reebok 63%. The time-reversed analysis calls into question Nike's claim because the latter results also illustrate Nike's "success." If we look more closely at the data, we see that the percentage of Nike consumers actually declined: from 64% at time 1 to 61% at time 2. Although more people stay with Nike, this is practically a statistical necessity because Nike has a larger share of the market. To test whether the percentage share is constant, we employ McNemar's test. We compare only the changers: there are 16 persons who switched to Nike versus the 21 who

TABLE 10.1. Time-Reversed Analysis of Brand Loyalty

	Time 2		
Time 1	Nike	Reebok	Total
Nike	73	21	94
Reebok	16	36	52
Total	89	57	146

Note. Adapted from Table 6.1 of Kenny and Campbell (1984). Copyright 1984 by Lawrence Erlbaum Associates. Adapted by permission.

switched away, the difference being –5. The appropriate test is $\chi^2(1) = (16 - 21)^2/21 + 16 = .68$, which is not statistically significant.

The results of McNemar's test satisfy the time-reversal criteria. In particular, the results of a time-reversed analysis—designating time 1 as time 2 and vice versa—will always be the opposite of the original analysis; that is, the number of those who "switched" to Nike is 21 and the number of those who "switched" away is 16, a difference of 5. When the original analysis indicates no change, so does the time-reversed analysis.

Several other statistical procedures can be shown to satisfy the time-reversal criteria; that is, when the flow of time is reversed, effect estimates reverse in sign and zero-effect estimates remain as 0. These methods include raw change score analysis (Chapter 5), standardized change score analysis (Chapter 5); univariate simplex (Chapter 8), quasi-simplex (Chapter 8), and trait–state–error (Chapter 8) models; and cross-lagged panel correlation (CLPC; Chapter 9). The reader might notice here that we have a peculiar fondness for preferring analysis methods that satisfy the time-reversal criteria.

Time-reversed analysis is an intriguing approach that we feel deserves further attention. However, it is not a cure-all for the analysis of longitudinal data. In certain cases a time-reversed analysis can yield inappropriate conclusions. If the regression discontinuity design (see Chapter 5) is employed and one uses the appropriate analysis (Reichardt, 1979; Trochim, 1984), a time-reversed analysis yields an inappropriate conclusion. Clearly, careful study is needed to determine when a time-reversed analysis is valid and when it is not.

Time-reversed analysis provides the researcher with a simple way of ruling out regression artifacts as a plausible alternative explanation of the results. To some it may seem to be an unjustifiable strategy in part because it supports what they see as questionable analysis strategies such as change score analysis and CLPC analysis. Rather, we believe that the principle of time reversal adds to the rationale for these procedures. We believe that employing a time-reversed analysis can add to the intuitive rationale for complex statistical analyses of over-time data, especially when regression toward the mean is a likely problem.

Statistical equating (multiple regression and partial correlation analysis) usually does not satisfy the time-reversal criteria. Nonetheless, we still urge a time-reversed analysis for this analysis technique. At the very least, the result should weaken under reversal; if it does not, we should be very suspicious as to the validity of the result.

One potential use for time-reversed models is the estimation of lagged effects in multilevel analysis. In these analyses, persons are measured at multiple time points and the over-time or lagged effect of one variable is measured. In a time-reversed analysis, the same analysis is undertaken but the flow of time is reversed. If the effect is real, then the effect in the time-reversed analysis should be much weaker.

GRAPHICAL DISPLAY OF RESULTS

Data analysis in the social and behavioral sciences has become increasingly complex in the last 20 years. Log-linear analysis, structural equation modeling, and hierarchical linear modeling are just some of the very complicated analyses that can be performed. In part, these more complicated analyses can now be performed because of the computational efficiency of computers. Analyses that used to take days to complete are now done in seconds after a few clicks of a computer mouse.

Although such analyses are useful and as methodologists we often strongly recommend these analytical techniques (as we did earlier in this chapter), we feel that many mistakes occur in these analyses because the researchers are not familiar with their data. The more complicated and less understood the analysis, the more likely that errors will be made, and so it becomes all the more necessary for researchers to become well acquainted with their data.

Researchers can become more familiar with their data by displaying them graphically. We have used scatter plots, which virtually all readers know about but most hardly ever use. We would urge that it become standard practice to draw the perfect-correlation lines when scatter plots are drawn. We have also introduced two new tools to illuminate regression artifacts: the pair-link and Galton squeeze diagrams. We strongly urge the use of these and other graphical techniques. The Galton squeeze diagram much more clearly illustrates regression toward the mean than does the more conventional scatter plot. We urge its use so that regression toward the mean can be more easily recognized and appreciated.

We have also introduced the concept of guesstimation. Instead of using a mathematical formula to compute a mean or draw a regression line, we just look at the data and guess at the value. Certainly, were we to publish the results of our analyses, we would not report guesstimates but would compute them. But in exploring data it helps to have a sense that the mathematical operations, like averages and slopes, have a meaning that can be readily seen in the data. Sometimes more can be learned from the data from inefficient and informal analyses than from complicated, exact, and optimal statistical analyses.

In this era of "point-and-click" data analysis, highly elaborate analyses can be performed in a matter of seconds. We would urge that programmers of commercial software include easy-to-use options for graphical displays. So, for instance, when a correlation coefficient is computed, a flashing message might urge the user to display a scatter plot, perferably with the perfect-correlation line.

Although we believe that sophisticated analyses of data are ordinarily needed, it is still necessary to explore the raw data in simple and direct ways. If the key result from a complicated analysis cannot be exhibited in the displays of raw data, then there should be skepticism about its very existence.

THE IMPORTANCE OF RESEARCH DESIGN

Given the recent advances in the statistical analysis of data, researchers have become able to perform very complicated statistical analyses of their data. However, data analysis, no matter how sophisticated, alone cannot solve inherent problems that are created by poor design. Students in the social sciences need to learn design principles as well as statistical techniques.

The most important design feature is randomization of persons to treatment groups. Although this primer has hardly discussed randomization, we are stalwart promoters of that procedure. Randomization provides the best way to make regression toward the mean implausible as a rival hypothesis. We recognize that randomization is not always possible, but we encourage its use whenever feasible. Complicated statistical analyses can seldom compensate for the benefits to internal validity afforded by random assignment of persons to treatment conditions.

Although randomization is the most important design feature, there are others that should also be considered. One critical feature is having a pretest. As we have shown (see especially Chapter 5), a pretest is not just another covariate. Rather, it has a special status that should be recognized in the statistical analysis (Campbell & Reichardt, 1991). With a pretest one may be able to calculate directly the degree of selection bias that is present in the outcome measure. That measure of selection bias can then be subtracted to obtain a relatively bias-free estimate of the intervention effect.

Another important design feature is random selection of persons in the research. As was shown in Chapter 3, random selection reduces but does not eliminate the plausible rival hypothesis of regression for the pre–post design. Random selection can also be an important way to increase the external validity of a study.

An excellent example of how statistical analysis cannot cure problems created by poor design is the unreliability of measures. With the development of latent variable analysis and computer programs like AMOS, CALIS, EQS, and LISREL, it is now possible to estimate models in which there is an allowance for errors of measurement in the predictor variables. Despite this statistical advance, it is still desirable to measure one's variables as reliably as possible. Estimates from models, either latent or not, are always better when more reliable measures are used. Moreover, models with variables with lots of measurement error are often not worth estimating, even with the most sophisticated latent variable modeling computer program.

Another important design principle is that of balance. Very often the optimal design is one in which there are equal numbers of persons in each cell of the design, an approach that accords with the principle of balance. It seems that with the ascendancy of multiple regression over analysis of variance, researchers have started to ignore balance in their designs, sometimes with disastrous consequences. A very unbalanced design leads to estimates that have very little precision.

A final point is that usually decisions made about the statistical analysis need to be based on aspects of the research design. Very often the choice between analysis methods rests not on statistical criteria but on the way the study is designed. Knowing how the data were collected is just as important as knowing complex statistical methods. The proper analysis of data requires that the analyst be well informed about the details of the design of the research.

CAREFUL CONSIDERATION OF
PLAUSIBLE RIVAL HYPOTHESES

A fundamental part of the analysis of data is the consideration and ideally the elimination of plausible rival hypotheses. This primer has focused on the most complex and perhaps most pervasive plausible rival hypothesis in over-time studies: regression toward the mean. Several texts (e.g., Campbell & Stanley, 1963; Cook & Campbell, 1979; Judd & Kenny, 1981) detail other explanations, such as history, selection, and maturation. Researchers need to consider alternative plausible explanations of the intervention effect and then attempt to show, as best they can, that such explanations are implausible.

All too often researchers fail to adequately consider counter explanations of their results. Instead they become advocates by hiding weaknesses of their research, dismissing too quickly criticisms of their work, and responding hostilely to questions from others. We feel that researchers have the responsibility to be their own worst critics of their work. As scientists, especially those among us who study human reasoning, we should know how easily we can make mistakes and delude ourselves about the correctness of our own position. Research conclusions need to be thoroughly probed and criticized by the investigator. After all, it is the investigator's scientific reputation that is at stake. The investigator should realize that an error will eventually be detected because the result will fail to replicate.

The one plausible rival hypothesis to which we have given special emphasis in this primer, besides regression toward the mean, is selection. Treatment "effects" very often reflect the effects of other variables that are not included in the analysis. Other literatures call this threat to validity "the omitted variable problem," "spuriousness," "the third variable problem," and "specification error." Especially in Chapters 4, 5, 8, and 9, we have argued that although statistical techniques such as multiple regression analysis reduce the bias due to selection, very often such bias persists. We urge researchers to concentrate their efforts to reduce the bias due to selection and to attempt to determine the direction of likely bias in their estimates. We worry that modern advances in data analysis (e.g., latent variable modeling and hierarchical linear modeling) do not in any way solve the problem of selection, but all too many researchers who use these methods seem to think that they do. Again, sophisticated data analysis cannot cover for the mistakes of poor design.

The term "plausible rival hypotheses" is used so much that its meaning may be lost. We need to emphasize that the expression contains the qualifier *plausible* (Campbell, 1969b). The researcher within a specific context makes a determination of plausibility. So what might be very plausible in some contexts might be implausible in another context. For instance, Campbell and Stanley (1963) considered the problem of pretest sensitization in attitude change research. They worried that by pretesting participants they would be sensitized to change when they read an attitude change message. However, research by Lana (1969) suggested that pretest sensitization effects are minimal, at least in the area of attitude change. So a testing by treatment interaction (i.e., pretest sensitization) is often not a very plausible rival hypothesis in attitude change research.

Sometimes a simple analysis can be performed to rule out a plausible rival hypothesis. For instance, if the worry were that the experimental participants might be more motivated than the control participants, then measuring whether there was a difference in motivation between the groups would be helpful. Occasionally, additional control groups can be used to render a plausible rival hypothesis implausible.

In over-time research without randomization, regression toward the mean is virtually always a plausible rival hypothesis that requires careful consideration. However, we want to caution the reader against the temptation to see regression toward the mean everywhere. This primer has carefully delineated how regression toward the mean works in different designs and contexts. Although often ignored and underappreciated, regression toward the mean does not explain every treatment effect that is observed. Moreover, as we explained in Chapters 4 and 5, certain analysis procedures overcorrect for the phenomenon. We can become artifact obsessed and lose sight of the fact that some phenomena are real and not just statistical artifacts. The good methodologist knows when to worry—and just as important when not to worry.

REGRESSION AND PREDICTION

Regression toward the mean can be used to improve the accuracy of predictions. Let us consider the predictions made by two hypothetical weather forecasters over a week. They each make seven predictions of the daily high temperature in their locality. These predictions can be compared to the actual daily high temperatures. Using a fairly common standard, we define an error in prediction as $Y - X$, where Y is the actual temperature and X the predicted temperature. Accuracy (actually inaccuracy) is defined as the sum of squared errors for the week. We refer to this measure as "accuracy," recognizing that the lower the number, the more accurate the forecaster.

The two sets of predictions and the actual temperatures are included in Table 10.2. Sally is quite an expert, and she achieves a very high correlation of .91 between her judgments and the actual

TABLE 10.2. Weather Predictions in Degrees Fahrenheit Made for a Week by Two Forecasters, Sal and Sally, and the Actual Temperatures

Day	Sal	Sally	Actual
Monday	50	57	53
Tuesday	50	52	48
Wednesday	50	59	53
Thursday	50	47	44
Friday	50	51	42
Saturday	50	67	56
Sunday	50	48	40
Mean	50	54.42	48
SD	0	7.07	6.19
Accuracy	258	343	

weather. Sal is a very lazy forecaster, but he knows that the average temperature in the locality is near 50 degrees Fahrenheit, and so he just predicts that the temperature will be 50 degrees every day of the week. It seems obvious that Sally should be more accurate than Sal. However, using the measure of accuracy that we introduced earlier, it is Sal who is more accurate! To understand why that is so, we need to understand better the factors that influence the accuracy of predictions.

Three different factors lead to errors in prediction: errors in the mean, errors in the rank order of responses, and errors of variance. When we naively think of errors, we tend to consider only errors about the rank order, but the other two types of errors are very important. Let us consider each of the three.

The first type of error concerns the discrepancy between the mean of the judgments and the mean of the criterion, or whether $M_X = M_Y$. A forecaster could have a perfect correlation with the actual temperature yet be off by 5 degrees Fahrenheit, and this constant error could considerably lower that forecaster's accuracy. In Table 10.2, we see that Sal is closer to the actual mean than Sally. This is the major reason why Sal is a more accurate forecaster than Sally.

The second error is the one that naive observers usually focus on most: the degree to which the forecaster reproduces the rank order. This type of error can be measured by how much the correlation between the forecast and the criterion measure is less than 1. Sally has a very impressive correlation of .91, and Sal has no correlation at all because there is no variability in his judgments.[3] It is for this reason that most observers would think Sally must be a better forecaster than Sal, but the other two reasons are important and more than offset this considerable advantage in the present case.

Finally, to maximize the accuracy of judgment, the standard deviation of the predictions should equal the standard deviation of the criterion times the correlation between the judgment and the criterion, or $s_X = r_{XY}s_Y$. (This condition implies that the slope using the judgments to predict the criterion equals 1.) It follows from this fact that the variance in predictions needs to be less than the variance of the criterion. Sally is a poor forecaster in that the variance of her predictions mirrors the variance in actual temperature. In fact, her judgments show slightly more variability than actual temperatures do. For optimal prediction, the standard deviation in the predictions should equal $r_{XY}s_Y$, or $(.91)(6.19) = 5.63$ for Sally. Her standard deviation is larger, 7.07, and that leads to increased inaccuracy of her predictions. As Kahneman and Tversky (1973) have demonstrated, if forecasters mistakenly try to make their judgments representative by matching variances, they are likely to be inaccurate. Although matching the mean of the criterion is good, matching the variance leads to increased errors. Optimal forecasting requires judicious use of regression toward the mean.[4]

There is one important special case for the condition of $s_X = r_{XY}s_Y$ that is worth noting. When r_{XY} equals 0, then it follows that the variance in the predictions should be 0. When the forecaster is totally ignorant, the best prediction is the mean with no variance in the judgments. If a forecaster does not know anything informative about the rank ordering of the objects of the predictions, he or she should just guess that they will all be average. So sometimes the best prediction is to guess that they are all the same, as Sal does.

The term that is used to describe that predictions should be less variable than what they are predicting is *shrinkage*. Unless there is perfect knowledge, the variance of predictions should be less than the variance of the variable being predicted. The less that a forecaster knows in terms of rank order, the more he or she should

---

[3]The denominator of the correlation contains the variance of Sal's predictions, and so it would be 0, making the correlation coefficient undefined.

[4]If we took Sally's predictions and transformed them as follows

$$.80(X - 54.42) + 48$$

she would outperform Sal, as her accuracy score would be 58.26.

shrink the variance in the predictions. The forecaster needs to regress his or her judgments toward the mean to increase the accuracy. To do this, the mean of the criterion to which the judgment is compared must be known.

So we can now understand why Sal outperforms Sally. Sal shrinks his judgments, perhaps a little too much. Sally fails to shrink her judgments in that the variability of her judgments is about the same as the variability of the criterion. The other reason for Sal's superiority as a forecaster is that he is much more accurate at knowing the mean than Sally. As this example shows, there is more to making accurate predictions than just getting the correlation right.

Shrinkage is used in statistical analyses that are sometimes called *empirical Bayes* estimates. One important use of empirical Bayes estimates is multilevel modeling (Bryk & Raudenbush, 1992). Within such models, the slopes (the effect of one variable on another) are estimated for each group of observations. For example, a slope is computed for children in each classroom. These estimated slopes for each classroom are shrunk to take into account regression toward the mean. The effect of this shrinkage is to reduce the variance in the estimated slopes, making each slope more similar to the average slope. The statistical estimates are regressed toward the mean estimate.

CONCLUSION

This chapter has summarized several themes echoed throughout this primer. After a brief epistemological exegesis that focused on the role of common sense, we have introduced a very useful procedure for diagnosing regression toward the mean: a time-reversed analysis. We have also discussed methods for improving the quality of research conclusions: the use of graphical methods, consideration of plausible rival hypotheses, and the importance of research design. Finally, we have shown how regression toward the mean should be incorporated into prediction.

We hope that by reading this chapter and the previous nine, the reader has learned about the concept of regression toward the mean. It can be a very confusing concept, and we have sought to clear up that confusion. The key idea is very simple: scores that are extreme in standard deviation units on one measure are not likely to be as extreme when measured on another measure. Complications arise in that to know whether there will be regression toward the mean depends on the process of selecting the score. Change is inevitable, but some components of scores change hardly at all; if selection is made on these components, there may be little or no regression to the mean. Forecasting the degree of regression toward the mean critically depends on an understanding of both the selection process that makes the score or mean of scores extreme and the model of change.

The reader might be surprised to learn that there is no statistical analysis that can remove or eliminate regression artifacts. Virtually all of the analyses that we have performed in this primer are standard analyses. We have the tools; we just need to use our intellect to use them in a way that reduces the likelihood of regression artifacts.

Regression toward the mean certainly deserves more attention than it has received in the recent past. It surprises us that this is the first book-length treatment of this most important topic. (It might well surprise others that a whole book has been written on this topic.)

More than a half century ago Rulon (1941) said, "The list of studies in which the regression factor has been neglected grows monotonous, as well as distressing" (p. 222). This dismal statement is included in virtually every review of regression toward the mean, and sadly this statement remains true today. We are hopeful that a few years from now, because of this primer and increased vigilance, Rulon's statement will no longer apply. We conclude with a more optimistic statement of Sir Francis Galton (1889), the man who coined the term "regression toward the mean":

> Some people hate the very name of statistics but I find them full of beauty and interest. Whenever they are not brutalized, but handled by higher methods, and are warily interpreted, their power of dealing with complicated phenomena is extraordinary. (p. 62)

Glossary of Terms

alpha: the probability of making a Type I error (rejecting the null hypothesis when it is true).

ANCOVA: the analysis of covariance; the analysis of variance with the addition of a continuous variable as a predictor variable.

ANOVA: the analysis of variance; a statistical technique to test hypothesis concerning the effects of categorical variables on a continuous variable.

anticompensatory program: program in which treatment participants outscore the control participants on pretreatment measures for which higher scores mean "better."

ARIMA model: autoregressive integrated moving average model for the analysis of time-series data.

assignment variable: variable correlated with the outcome and used to assign persons to treatment groups; the source of nonrandomized selection effects.

autocorrelation: in a time series, the degree of correlation between two time points separated by a fixed length of time or lag.

autocorrelogram: a graph of the strength of autocorrelation as a function of lag length.

autoregressive coefficient: coefficient indicating the degree to which the current value is influenced by the previous value.

autoregressive model: for time-series and longitudinal data, a model in which the current value is assumed to be a function of the previous values plus a random component.

blocking: matching using a categorical variable; term often used in randomized experiments.

caliper matching: matching on a continuous variable, with an interval defined for which persons are "similar enough" for an acceptable match.

change score analysis: method using change as the outcome in over-time analyses.

Cohen's *d*: mean difference between two treatment groups divided by the pooled within-groups standard deviation; a measure of effect size.

compensatory program: program in which control participants outscore the treatment participants on pretreatment measures for which higher scores mean "better."

construct validity: validity when the measure actually taps the intended theoretical construct.

control group: persons who have not received the treatment and to whom the treated group is compared.

correlation: the degree of linear association between two standardized variables; the slope divided by the perfect slope; ranges from -1 to $+1$; measure of effect size.

covariate: a measure that is correlated with the outcome but not affected by the treatment or the outcome.

cross-lagged panel correlation (CLPC): a method for ruling out the plausible rival hypothesis of spuriousness using longitudinal data.

cycle: in a time series, a recurrence of observations separated by a constant interval that tend to be similar to one another.

effect size: the magnitude of the standardized effect of a treatment variable on an outcome.

error variance: in psychometrics, the variance in a measure not due to true variance, estimated by the measure's variance times 1 minus the measure's reliability; alternatively in modeling, the unexplained variance in a variable.

external validity: the generalizability of the results from a study; a threat to such validity is the interaction of treatment with another variable.

Galton squeeze diagram: a pair-link diagram in which the levels of one variable are connected to the means of the other variable.

growth-curve model: a model in which change is determined by time but the rates and starting points of change may vary by individual.

guesstimate: an approximation through a visual examination, not a mathematical computation, of a statistic (e.g., a mean or slope).

history: the plausible rival hypothesis that a change in an outcome is due to some intervening event and not the treatment.

horizontal squeeze plot: a scatter plot in which means or guesstimates are computed for each value on the variable on the vertical axis; the scatter plot is squeezed horizontally.

instrumentation: the plausible rival hypothesis that a change in an outcome is due to a change in the calibration of the measuring device, not the treatment.

internal validity: valid causal inference (threatened by plausible rival hypotheses such as regression toward the mean).

interrupted time-series design: a time series in which the initial observations serve as the control and, after an intervention is introduced, the remaining observations are treated.

lag: the time interval between measurements.

latent variable: a theoretical construct that is imperfectly measured by one or more indicators.

linearity: the assumption that the relationship between two variables can be best fitted by a straight line.

Lord's paradox: when treatment groups differ on a pretreatment measure, covarying out that measure and change score analysis yield different conclusions.

matching: measuring the treatment effect across equivalent scores on a third variable to reduce, but likely not eliminate, bias due to selection.

maturation: the plausible rival hypothesis that a change in an outcome is due to development and not the treatment.

measurement error: the random, unsystematic component in a measurement.

mega-covariate: a covariate that is formed by combining the values of two or more covariates.

mortality: the plausible rival hypothesis that persons who leave the treatment and control groups do so for different reasons; a type of selection effect.

multilevel modeling: a statistical method for the analysis of data at two or more levels (e.g., children and classrooms, or persons and times).

multiple regression: a statistical technique for the simultaneous estimation of the effects of several predictors that add together.

multitrait–multimethod matrix (MTMM): a correlation matrix between a set of variables (i.e., traits) all measured by the same set of methods.

nonequivalent control group design: a research design in which treatment and control groups are nonrandomly formed and persons are pre- and posttested.

null hypothesis: the hypothesis that some population value (e.g., a mean difference, a correlation, or a regression coefficient) equals some particular value (usually 0).

omitted variable: a variable not controlled in the statistical analysis that causes the outcome and the assignment variable; the assignment variable; the source of selection effects.

overadjustment: biasing of the estimated treatment in the direction of the difference on the covariate (the covariate being scaled to correlate positively with the outcome).

overfitted regression line: if X is used to predict Y, the line by which the predicted values of Y for each value of X are plotted and connected.

pair-link diagram: graph of a two-variable association; two vertical lines, one for each variable, with each pair of scores represented by a line connecting these two vertical lines.

parallel test: a second measure of the same construct that has the same amount of true and error variance and sometimes is assumed to have the same mean.

perfect-correlation line: a slope of the standard deviation of the criterion divided by the standard deviation of the predictor; when units of measurement the same, a diagonal line.

phantom variable: a variable in a model that has no substantive meaning but is used as a vehicle for forcing a constraint (e.g., a nonlinear constraint in structural equation modeling).

plausible rival hypothesis: a threat to internal validity; an alternative explanation of the treatment effect.

power: the probability of rejecting the null hypothesis; 1 minus the probability of making a Type II error.

pre–post design: a research design in which a group of persons is measured before and after receiving a treatment.

pretest: a prior measure of the outcome.

proximal autocorrelation: the outcome when the correlation between shorter time lags is larger than the correlation between longer lags.

quasi-simplex: a simplex correlational structure that is attenuated by measurement error.

random assignment: the assignment of persons into treatment groups by a random rule; such persons have a fixed probability of being assigned to a given treatment group.

randomized experiments: studies in which units, typically persons, are randomly assigned to treatments.

random selection: the selection of persons into a study randomly from some specified population.

regression discontinuity design: a research design in which persons are assigned to treatment groups on the basis of a measured variable.

regression line: if X is used to predict Y, the line that minimizes the sum of squared errors of prediction.

regression toward the mean: because of a less than perfect correlation, the predicted score of a variable tends to be not as extreme in terms of standard score units as is the predictor variable in standard score units.

reliability: the proportion of variance in a measure that is true, commonly estimated by an internal consistency measure.

scatter plot: a graph in which the axes are two variables and the points represent the scores of individuals on the variables.

selection: the plausible rival hypothesis that the treatment difference is due to a preexisting difference on some unknown variable; that unknown variable is called the assignment variable.

selection by maturation: persons at the different levels of the assignment variable are changing at different rates.

selection by regression: persons at the different levels of the assignment variable are regressing to different means.

shrinkage: the variance of predicted scores using the standard regression prediction formula must be less than or equal to the variance of the observed scores; how much less depends on the correlation between the prediction and the score being predicted.

simplex: the correlational structure that results from a first-order autoregressive model; the resulting structure is proximally autocorrelated.

spuriousness: the covariation between two variables that is not due to one causing the other, but rather to the variables both being caused by a third variable.

standardization: the transformation of a variable so that its mean is 0 and its variance is 1; Z scoring.

standardized change score analysis: the method by which the components of a change score have equal variance through standardization; the formula for this analysis is $Y - (s_Y/s_X)X$.

stationarity: the condition when parameters do not change over time (e.g., the mean and the standard deviations of the pretest and the posttest are the same).

statistical equating: a method using multiple regression in an attempt to control presumed selection variables.

structural equation modeling: models with causal links between latent or unmeasured variables.

synchronous correlation: the correlation between two variables measured at the same time.

testing: the plausible rival hypothesis that the process of being measured affects subsequent measurements.

time-reversed analysis: the analysis of data by switching the flow of time and determining if the results change.

time series: data from a single unit that are temporally ordered.

trait–state–error model: a model of change with three components: a trait or unchanging component, a state or autoregressive component, and an error or random component.

treatment: an intervention or program; the variable that contrasts the two groups in an evaluation.

trend: a constant change in a variable over time.

true-score estimate: an estimate in which, given an observed score, the predicted true score is regressed or shrunk toward the mean using the formula $M_X + r_X(X - M_X)$, where r_X is the measure's reliability.

true variance: the portion of variance in a measure that is not error; estimated by the measure's variance times its reliability.

Type I error: the error of rejecting the null hypothesis when it is true; its probability is denoted as alpha.

Type II error: the error of not rejecting the null hypothesis when it is false; its probability is denoted as beta; power equals 1 minus beta.

underadjustment: biasing of the estimated treatment in the direction opposite from the difference on the covariate (the covariate being scaled to correlate positively with the outcome).

vertical squeeze plot: a scatter plot in which means or guesstimates are computed for each value of the variable on the horizontal axis; the scatter plot is squeezed vertically.

zero-correlation line: a flat line that intersects the mean of the variable being predicted.

Glossary of Symbols

X pretest or one of the variables in CLPC

Y posttest or one of the variables in CLPC

X' predicted pretest given the posttest

Y' predicted posttest given the pretest

Z_X standardized pretest

Z_Y standardized posttest

Z'_X predicted standardized pretest given the posttest

Z'_Y predicted standardized posttest given the pretest

X_T pretest true score

Y_T posttest true score

X'_T estimated pretest true score

Y'_T estimated posttest true score

M mean

M_T mean of the treated group

M_C mean of the control group

M_X mean of the pretest

M_Y mean of the posttest

s standard deviation

s_X standard deviation of the pretest

s_Y standard deviation of the posttest

r correlation coefficient

r_{XY} correlation of the pretest and the posttest

b_{YX} regression coefficient in which the posttest is predicted by the pretest

b_{XY} regression coefficient in which the pretest is predicted by the posttest

r_1 the lag-1 autocorrelation

r_k the lag-k autocorrelation

X_1 measurement at wave 1

X_2 measurement at wave 2

r_{12} the correlation between measurements at wave 1 and wave 2

r_X reliability of the pretest

r_Y reliability of the posttest

APPENDIX A

Dice-Rolling Program and Data Sets Used as Illustrations

Readers can access the computer program that was used to generate much of the data and graphs used in this primer from the following World-Wide Web address:

htpp://nw3.nai.net/~dakenny/primer.htm

The computer program, called RTM (regression toward the mean), generates a pretest and posttest for a group of persons. (Should the website change, readers should search for "primer" and "RTM.") The user can specify the number of cases. Each score is based on one to four dice rolls, and all, some, or none of the dice rolls can be shared. By sharing more dice, the correlation's size can be increased. Negative correlations can be created by subtracting the shared dice, and this can be accomplished by entering a negative number of shared dice. A number from 1 to 4 can be added to either the pretest or the posttest. The data set that is created can be stored for subsequent analysis.

The correlation between pretest and posttest equals the number of dice shared divided by the square root of the product of the number of dice rolled at the pre- and posttest. If the number of shared dice is negative, the correlation is negative. So, for instance, if 2 dice are thrown at the pretest, 4 dice are thrown at the posttest, and 2 dice are shared, the correlation is 2 divided by the square root of 8, which equals .707. If 3 dice are thrown at both the pretest and posttest and –1 die is shared, the correlation is –1 divided by the square root of 9, which equals –.333.

Output from the program include basic statistics, histograms, scatter plots, overfitted regression lines, and Galton squeeze diagrams. The overfitted lines and the Galton squeeze diagrams are given forward and backward in time. The user can control what output is presented.

The website also includes the major data sets used in this primer. The data sets can be downloaded from the website and reanalyzed by RTM. The computer program is written in QuickBASIC and runs on IBM-compatible personal computers.

The website will contain updates and errata for this primer. Readers can send corrections and suggestions to the second author through the website.

APPENDIX B

The Computation of Autocorrelations

Consider a very short time series of

$$4, 3, 4, 7, 5, 8, 6, 7, 8, 8$$

To compute the autocorrelation, we first lag the time series. The series and the lagged series are presented below:

$$
\begin{array}{cccccccccc}
4, & 3, & 4, & 7, & 5, & 8, & 6, & 7, & 8, & 8 \\
| & | & | & | & | & | & | & | & | \\
4, & 3, & 4, & 7, & 5, & 8, & 6, & 7, & 8, & 8
\end{array}
$$

The covariation between the paired observations (e.g., 3–4, 4–3, 7–4, and so on) is then observed. The formula for the lag-1 autocorrelation is

$$\frac{\Sigma(X_i - M_X)(X_{i+1} - M_X)}{\Sigma(X_i - M_X)^2}$$

where M_X is the mean of all the observations. So, for the example, the lag-1 autocorrelation equals .41.

The general formula for the lag-k autocorrelation is

$$\frac{\Sigma(X_i - M_X)(X_{i+k} - M_X)}{\Sigma(X_i - M_X)^2}$$

Notice that there are k fewer terms on the numerator than there are in the denominator, in that the summation goes from 1 to $N - k$, where N is the number of observations. The lag-2 through the lag-5 autocorrelations for the example data are .28, .00, –.03, and –.19, respectively. If there were trends and cycles in the series, then the observations would be first detrended and decycled before the autocorrelations were computed.

These standard formulas for autocorrelations are negatively biased; that is, they underestimate the population autocorrelation. We present an alternative formula for the lag-1 autocorrelation proposed by Huitema and McKean (1994). It takes the following form:

$$\frac{[.5[(X_1 - M_X)^2 + (X_N - M_X)^2] + \Sigma[(X_i - M_X)(X_{i+1} - M_X)]] \, [1 + 5/(N-1)]}{\Sigma(X_i - M_X)^2}$$

where again N is the number of observations. For the example data, the lag-1 autocorrelation equals .83. Note that this value is nearly three times as large as the value obtained using the standard estimation method. Based on simulations, if the true correlation were .80 and N were 10, the standard value would be estimated to be .35 and this modified value would be .71. Clearly the Huitema and McKean (1994) modification reduces the bias in the estimation of the lag-1 autocorrelation.

References

Abelson, R. P. (1995). *Statistics as principled argument*. Mahwah, NJ: Erlbaum.

Andrews, G., & Harvey, R. (1981). Regression toward the mean in pretreatment measures of stuttering. *Journal of Speech and Hearing Disorders, 46*, 204–207.

Anthony, J. C., LeResche, L., Niaz, U., Von Korff, M. R., & Folstein, M. F. (1982). Limits of the "Mini-Mental State" as a screening for dementia and delirium among hospital patients. *Psychological Medicine, 12*, 397–408.

Ashenfelter, O. (1978). Estimating the effect of training programs on earnings. *Review of Economics and Statistics, 60*, 47–57. [Reprinted 1980 in E. W. Stromsdorfer & G. Farkas (Eds.), *Evaluation studies review annual* (Vol. 5, pp. 307–317). Beverly Hills, CA: Sage.]

Baltes, P. B., Nesselroade, J. R., Schaie, K. W., & Labouvie, E. W. (1972). On the dilemma of regression effects in examining ability-level-related differentials in ontogenetic patterns of intelligence. *Developmental Psychology, 6*, 78–84.

Bohrnstedt, G. W. (1969). Observations on the measurement of change. In E. F. Borgatta (Ed.), *Sociological methodology 1969* (pp. 113–133). San Francisco: Jossey-Bass.

Brewer, M. B., Campbell, D. T., & Crano, W. D. (1970). Testing a single factor model as an alternative to the misuse of partial correlations in hypothesis-testing research. *Sociometry, 33*, 1–11.

Bryk, A. S., & Raudenbush, S. W. (1992). *Hierarchical linear models: Applications and data analysis methods*. Newbury Park, CA: Sage.

Calsyn, R., & Kenny, D. A. (1977). Self-concept of ability and perceived evaluation of others: Cause or effect of academic achievement? *Journal of Educational Psychology, 69*, 136–145.

Campbell, D. T. (1963). From description to experimentation: Interpreting trends as quasi-experiments. In C. W. Harris (Ed.), *Problems in measuring change* (pp. 212–242). Madison: University of Wisconsin.

Campbell, D. T. (1969a). Reforms as experiments. *American Psychologist,* 24, 409–429. [Reprinted 1988 in *Methodology and epistemology for social science* (E. S. Overman, Ed., pp. 261–289). Chicago: University of Chicago Press.]

Campbell, D. T. (1969b). Prospective: Artifact and control. In R. Rosenthal & R. L. Rosnow (Eds.), *Artifact in behavioral research* (pp. 351–382). New York: Academic Press.

Campbell, D. T. (1974). Evolutionary epistemology. In P. A. Schilpp (Ed.), *The philosophy of Karl Popper* (pp. 413–463). LaSalle, IL: Open Court. [Reprinted 1988 in *Methodology and epistemology for social science* (E. S. Overman, Ed., pp. 393–434). Chicago: University of Chicago Press.]

Campbell, D. T. (1975). Assessing the impact of planned social change. In G. M. Lyons (Ed.), *Social research and public policies* (an OECD Conference) (pp. 3–45). Hanover, NH: Public Affairs Center, Dartmouth College. [Reprinted 1979 in *Evaluation and Program Planning,* 2, 67–90.]

Campbell, D. T. (1988). *Methodology and epistemology for social science* (E. S. Overman, Ed.). Chicago: University of Chicago Press.

Campbell, D. T. (1994). Retrospective and prospective on program impact assessment. *Evaluation Practice, 15,* 291–298.

Campbell, D. T. (1996). Regression artifacts in time-series and longitudinal data. *Evaluation and Program Planning, 19,* 377–389.

Campbell, D. T., & Boruch, R. F. (1975). Making the case for randomized assignment to treatments by considering the alternatives: Six ways in which quasi-experimental evaluations in compensatory education tend to underestimate effects. In C. A. Bennett & A. Lumsdaine (Eds.), *Evaluation and experiments: Some critical issues in assessing social programs* (pp. 195–296). New York: Academic Press.

Campbell, D. T., & Clayton, K. N. (1961). Avoiding regression effects in panel studies of communication impact. *Studies in Public Communication, 3,* 99–118.

Campbell, D. T., & Erlebacher, A. (1970). How regression artifacts in quasi-experimental evaluations can mistakenly make compensatory education look harmful. In J. Hellmuth (Ed.), *Compensatory education: A national debate: Vol. 3. Disadvantaged child* (pp. 185–225). New York: Brunner/Mazel.

Campbell, D. T., & Fiske, D. W. (1959). Convergent and discriminant validation by the multitrait–multimethod matrix. *Psychological Bulletin, 56,* 81–105.

Campbell, D. T., & Reichardt, C. S. (1983, June 5–8). *Quasi-experimental forecasting of the impact of planned interventions.* Paper presented at the Third International Symposium on Forecasting, Philadelphia, PA.

Campbell, D. T., & Reichardt, C. S. (1991). Problems in assuming the comparability of pretest and posttest in autoregressive and growth models. In R. E. Snow & D. Wiley (Eds.), *Improving inquiry in social science: A volume in honor of Lee J. Cronbach* (pp. 201–219). Mahwah, NJ: Erlbaum.

Campbell, D. T., & Ross, H. L. (1968). The Connecticut crackdown on speeding: Time-series data in quasi-experimental analysis. *Law and Society Review, 3,* 33–53.

Campbell, D. T., & Stanley, J. C. (1963). Experimental and quasi-experimental designs for research on teaching. In N. L. Gage (Ed.), *Handbook of research on teaching* (pp. 171–246). Chicago: Rand McNally. [Reprinted 1966 as *Experimental and quasi-experimental designs for research.* Boston: Houghton Mifflin.]

Campbell, D. T., & Thistlethwaite, D. L. (1960). Regression-discontinuity analysis: An alternative to the ex post facto experiment. *Journal of Educational Psychology, 51,* 309–317.

Cappelleri, J. C., Trochim, W. M., Stanley, T. D., & Reichardt, C. S. (1991). Random measurement error does not bias the treatment effect estimate in the regression-discontinuity design: I. The case of no interaction. *Evaluation Review, 15,* 395–419.

Chen, M. K. (1967). A critical look at the matching technique in experimentation. *Journal of Experimental Education, 35,* 95–98.

Cohen, J. (1988). *Statistical power analysis for the behavioral sciences* (2nd ed.). Mahwah, NJ: Erlbaum.

Cohen, J., & Cohen, P. (1983). *Applied multiple regression and correlation analysis for the behavioral sciences* (2nd ed.). Mahwah, NJ: Erlbaum.

Coleman, S. P. (1994). *Contribution of method-facet types to model appropriateness in the analysis of multitrait–multimethod matrices.* Unpublished doctoral dissertation, University of Denver.

Collins, L. M. (1996). Is reliability obsolete?: A commentary on "Are simple gain scores obsolete?" *Applied Psychological Measurement, 20,* 289–292.

Collins, L. M., & Horn, J. L. (Eds.). (1991). *Best methods for the analysis of change: Recent advances, unanswered questions, future direction.* Washington, DC: American Psychological Association.

Cook, T. D., & Campbell, D. T. (1979). *Quasi-experimentation: Design and analysis for field settings.* Boston: Houghton Mifflin.

Crano, W., Kenny, D. A., & Campbell, D. T. (1972). Does intelligence cause achievement?: A cross-lagged panel analysis. *Journal of Educational Psychology, 63,* 258–275.

Cronbach, L. J., & Furby, L. (1970). How we should measure "change"— or should we? *Psychological Bulletin, 74,* 68–80. [See also Errata, *ibid.,* 1970, 74, 218.]

Cronbach, L. J., Gleser, G. C., Nanda, H., & Rajaratnam, N. (1972). *The dependability of behavioral measurements: Theory of generalizability for scores and profiles.* New York: Wiley.

Cudeck, R. (1989). The analysis of correlation matrices using covariance structure models. *Psychological Bulletin, 105,* 317–327.

Cummings, N. A., & Follette, W. T. (1968). Brief psychotherapy and medical utilization in a prepaid health plan setting: Part II. *Medical Care, 6*, 31–41.

Cummings, N. A., & Follette, W. T. (1976). Brief psychotherapy and medical utilization: An eight year follow-up. In H. Dorken & Associates (Eds.), *The professional psychologist today: New developments in law, health insurance, and health practice* (pp. 165–174). San Francisco: Jossey-Bass.

Cutter, G. R. (1976). Some examples for teaching regression toward the mean from a sampling viewpoint. *American Statistician, 30*, 194–197.

Davis, C. E. (1976). The effect of regression toward the mean in epidemiological and clinical studies. *American Journal of Epidemiology, 104*, 493–498.

Director, S. M. (1979). Underadjustment bias in the evaluation of manpower training. *Evaluation Quarterly, 3*, 190–218.

Dubois, P. H. (1957). *Multivariate correlational analysis.* New York: Harper.

Duncan, O. D. (1969). Some linear models for two-wave, two-variable panel analysis. *Psychological Bulletin, 72*, 177–182.

Duncan, O. D. (1972). Unmeasured variables in linear models for panel analysis: Some didactic examples. In H. L. Costner (Ed.), *Sociological methodology 1972* (pp. 36–82). San Francisco: Jossey-Bass.

Dunham, W. (1994). *The mathematical universe.* New York: Wiley.

Dwyer, J. H. (1986). *A model of entropic decay.* Unpublished manuscript, University of Southern California, Los Angeles.

Epstein, E., & Guttman, R. (1984). Mate selection in man: Evidence, theory, and outcome. *Social Biology, 31*, 243–278.

Fleiss, J. L. (1976). Comment on Overall and Woodward's asserted paradox concerning the measurement of change. *Psychological Bulletin, 83*, 774–775.

Flett, G. L., Vredenburg, K., & Krames, L. (1995). The stability of depressive symptoms in college students: An empirical demonstration of regression to the mean. *Journal of Psychopathology and Behavioral Assessment, 17*, 403–415.

Follette, W., & Cummings, N. A. (1967). Psychiatric services and medical utilization in a prepaid health plan setting: Part I. *Medical Care, 5*, 25–35.

Furby, L. (1973). Interpreting regression toward the mean in developmental research. *Developmental Psychology, 8*, 172–179.

Furlong, M. J., & Feldman, M. G. (1992). Can ability–achievement regression toward the mean account for MDT discretionary decisions? *Psychology in the Schools, 29*, 205–212.

Galton, F. (1879). Typical laws of heredity. *Proceedings of the Royal Institute of Great Britain (Proceedings for the years 1875–1878)*, pp. 282–301.

Galton, F. (1886). Regression towards mediocrity in hereditary stature. *Journal of the Anthropological Institute of Great Britain and Ireland, 15*, 246–263.

Galton, F. (1889). *Natural inheritance*. London: Macmillan.

Gibbons, R. D., Hedeker, D., & Davis, J. M. (1987). Regression toward the mean: More on the price of beer and the salaries of priests. *Psychoneuroendocrinology, 12*, 185–192.

Gilovich, T. (1991). *How we know what isn't so: The fallibility of human reason in everyday life*. New York: Free Press.

Glock, C. Y. (1951). Some applications of the panel method to the study of change. *American Society for Testing Materials, Symposium on Measurement of Consumer Wants, Special Technical Publication No. 117, 46–54*. [Reprinted 1955 in P. F. Lazarsfeld & M. Rosenberg (Eds.), *The language of social research* (pp. 231–242). Glencoe, IL: Free Press.]

Gottman, J. M. (1995). *The analysis of change*. Mahwah, NJ: Erlbaum.

Gottman, J. M., & Rushe, R. H. (1993). The analysis of change: Issues, fallacies, and new ideas. *Journal of Consulting and Clinical Psychology, 61*, 907–910.

Harris, C. W. (1963). *Problems in measuring change*. Madison: University of Wisconsin.

Harrison, J. R., & Bazerman, M. H. (1995). Regression toward the mean, expectation inflation, and the winner's curse in organizational contexts. In *Negotiation as a social process: New trends in theory and research* (pp. 69–94). Thousand Oaks, CA: Sage.

Hays, W. L. (1963). *Statistics*. New York: Holt, Rinehart & Winston.

Heimendinger, J., & Laird, N. (1983). Growth changes: Measuring the effect of an intervention. *Evaluation Review, 7*, 80–95.

Heise, D. R. (1970). Causal inference from panel data. In E. F. Borgatta & G. W. Bohrnstedt (Eds.), *Sociological methodology 1970* (pp. 3–27). San Francisco: Jossey-Bass.

Hooker, R. H. (1901). Correlation of the marriage rate with trade. *Journal of the Royal Statistical Society, 64*, 485–492.

Huitema B. E. (1985). Autocorrelation in applied behavioral analysis: A myth. *Journal of Behavioral Assessment, 7*, 107–118.

Huitema, B. E., & McKean, J. W. (1994). Two reduced-bias autocorrelation estimators: r_{F1} and r_{F2}. *Perceptual and Motor Skills, 78*, 323–330.

Humphreys, L. G. (1960). Investigations of the simplex. *Psychometrika, 25*, 313–323.

Humphreys, L. G. (1986). Commentary. *Journal of Vocational Behavior, 29*, 421–437.

Humphreys, L. G. (1996). Linear dependence of gain scores on their components imposes constraints on their use and interpretation: Comment on "Are simple gain scores obsolete?" *Applied Psychological Measurement, 20*, 293–294.

Humphreys, L. G., & Drasgow, F. (1989). Some comments on the relation between reliability and statistical power. *Applied Psychological Measurement, 13*, 419–425.

Jones, K., & Vischi, T. (1979). Impact of alcohol, drug abuse, and mental health treatment on medical care utilization: A review of the research literature. *Medical Care, 17*, i–vi, 1–82.

Judd, C. M., & Kenny, D. A. (1981). *Estimating the effects of social interventions.* Cambridge, England: Cambridge University Press.

Kahneman, D., & Tversky, A. (1973). On the psychology of prediction. *Psychological Review, 80*, 237–251.

Kenny, D. A. (1973). Cross-lagged and synchronous common factors in panel data. In A. S. Goldberger & O. D. Duncan (Eds.), *Structural equation models in the social sciences* (pp. 153–166). New York: Seminar Press.

Kenny, D. A. (1975a). A quasi-experimental approach to assessing treatment effects in the nonequivalent control group design. *Psychological Bulletin, 82*, 345–362.

Kenny, D. A. (1975b). Cross-lagged panel correlation: A test for spuriousness. *Psychological Bulletin, 82*, 887–903.

Kenny, D. A. (1979). *Correlation and causality.* New York: Wiley-Interscience.

Kenny, D. A., & Campbell, D. T. (1984). Methodological considerations in the analysis of temporal data. In K. Gergen & M. Gergen (Eds.), *Historical social psychology* (pp. 125–138). Mahwah, NJ: Erlbaum.

Kenny, D. A., & Campbell, D. T. (1989). On the measurement of stability in over-time data. *Journal of Personality, 57*, 445–481.

Kenny, D. A., & Cohen, S. H. (1980). A reexamination of selection and growth processes in the nonequivalent control group design. In K. F. Scheussler (Ed.), *Sociological methodology 1980* (pp. 290–313). San Francisco: Jossey-Bass.

Kenny, D. A., & Harackiewicz, J. M. (1979). Cross-lagged panel correlation: Practice and promise. *Journal of Applied Psychology, 64*, 372–379.

Kenny, D. A., Kieffer, S. C., Smith, J. A., Ceplinski, P., & Kulo, J. (1996). Circumscribed accuracy among well-acquainted individuals. *Journal of Experimental Social Psychology, 32*, 1–12.

Kenny, D. A., & Nasby, W. (1980). Splitting the reciprocity correlation. *Journal of Personality and Social Psychology, 38*, 249–256.

Kenny, D. A., & Zaccaro, S. J. (1983). An estimate of variance due to traits in leadership. *Journal of Applied Psychology, 68*, 678–685.

Kenny, D. A., & Zautra, A. (1995). The trait–state–error model for multiwave data. *Journal of Consulting and Clinical Psychology, 63*, 52–59.

Kline, R. B. (1998). *Principles and practice of structural equation modeling.* New York: Guilford Press.

Kogan, W. S., Thompson, D. J., Brown, J. R., & Newman, H. F. (1975). Impact of integration of mental health service and comprehensive medical care. *Medical Care, 13*, 934.

Lana, R. E. (1969). Pretest sensitization. In R. Rosenthal & R. L. Rosnow (Eds.), *Artifact in behavioral research* (pp. 119–141). New York: Academic Press.

Lazarsfeld, P. F. (1972). Mutual effects of statistical variables. In P. F. Lazarsfeld, A. K. Pasanella, & M. Rosenberg (Eds.), *Continuities in the language of social research*. New York: Free Press.

Lefkowitz, M. M., Eron, L. D. Walder, L. O., & Huesmann, L. R. (1972). Television violence and child aggression: A follow-up study. In G. A. Comstock & E. A. Rubinstein (Eds.), *Television and social behavior* (Vol. 3, pp. 35–135). Washington, DC: U.S. Government Printing Office.

Levesque, M. J., & Kenny, D. A. (1993). Accuracy of behavioral predictions at zero acquaintance: A social relations analysis. *Journal of Personality and Social Psychology, 65,* 1178–1187.

Levin, J. R. (1982). Modifications of a regression-toward-the-mean demonstration. *Teaching of Psychology, 9,* 237–238.

Lord, F. M. (1956). The measurement of growth. *Educational and Psychological Measurement, 16,* 421–437. [See also Errata, *ibid.,* 1957, *17,* 452.]

Lord, F. M. (1958). Further problems in the measurement of growth. *Educational and Psychological Measurement, 18,* 437–454.

Lord, F. M. (1960). Large-sample covariance analysis when the control variable is fallible. *Journal of the American Statistical Association, 55,* 309–321.

Lord, F. M. (1963). Elementary models for measuring change. In C. W. Harris (Ed.), *Problems in measuring change* (pp. 199–211). Madison: University of Wisconsin Press.

Lord, F. M. (1967). A paradox in the interpretation of group comparisons. *Psychological Bulletin, 68,* 304–305.

Lund, T. (1989a). The statistical regression phenomenon: I. A metamodel. *Scandinavian Journal of Psychology, 30,* 2–11.

Lund, T. (1989b). The statistical regression phenomenon: II. Application of a metamodel. *Scandinavian Journal of Psychology, 30,* 12–29.

MacCallum, R. C., Wegener, D. T., Uchino, B. N., & Fabrigar, L. R. (1993). The problem of equivalent models in applications of covariance structure analysis. *Psychological Bulletin, 114,* 185–199.

Mann, R. D. (1959). A review of the relationships between personality and performance in small groups. *Psychological Bulletin, 56,* 241–270.

Mark, M. M. (1986). Validity typologies and the logic and practice of quasi-experimentation. In M. K. Trochim (Ed.), *Advances in quasi-experimental design and analysis: New directions for program evaluation, No. 31* (pp. 47–66). San Francisco: Jossey-Bass.

Mark, M. M., & Mellor, S. (1991). Effect of self-relevance of an event on hindsight bias: The foreseeability of a layoff. *Journal of Applied Psychology, 76,* 569–577.

Maxwell, S. E., Delaney, H. D., & Dill, C. A. (1984). Another look at ANCOVA versus blocking. *Psychological Bulletin, 95,* 136–147.

McArdle, J. J., & Epstein, D. (1987). Latent growth curves within developmental structural equation models. *Child Development, 58,* 110–133.

McCain, L. J., & McCleary, R. (1979). The statistical analysis of the simple interrupted time-series design. In T. D. Cook & D. T. Campbell, *Quasi-experimentation: Design and analysis for field settings* (pp. 233–293). Boston: Houghton Mifflin.

McNemar, Q. (1940). A critical examination of the University of Iowa studies of environmental influences upon the I.Q. *Psychological Bulletin, 37,* 63–92.

McNemar, Q. (1958). On growth measurement. *Educational and Psychological Measurement, 18,* 47–55.

Milich, R., Roberts, M. A., Loney, J., & Caputo, J. (1980). Differentiating practice effects and statistical regression on the Conners Hyperactivity Index. *Journal of Abnormal Child Psychology, 8,* 549–552.

Millsap, R. E. (1995). The statistical analysis of method effects in multitrait–multimethod data: A review. In P. E. Shrout & S. T. Fiske (Eds.), *Personality research, methods, and theory: A Festschrift honoring Donald W. Fiske* (pp. 93–110). Mahwah, NJ: Erlbaum.

Mullen, B., & Cooper, C. (1994). The relation between cohesiveness and productivity: An integration. *Psychological Bulletin, 115,* 210–227.

Nesselroade, J. R., Stigler, S. M., & Baltes, P. B. (1980). Regression toward the mean and the study of change. *Psychological Bulletin, 88,* 622–637.

Newcomb, T. M. (1979). Reciprocity of interpersonal attraction: A nonconfirmation of a plausible hypothesis. *Social Psychology Quarterly, 42,* 299–306.

Nicewander, W. A., & Price, J. M. (1978). Dependent variable reliability and the power of significance tests. *Psychological Bulletin, 85,* 405–409.

Olbrisch, M. E. (1977). Psychotherapeutic interventions in physical health: Effectiveness and economic efficiency. *American Psychologist, 32,* 761–777.

Olbrisch, M. E. (1980). Psychological intervention and reduced medical care utilization: A modest interpretation. *American Psychologist, 35,* 760–761.

Overall, J. E., & Woodward, J. A. (1975). Unreliability of difference scores: A paradox for measurement of change. *Psychological Bulletin, 82,* 85–86.

Patterson, D. Y., & Bise, B. (1978, January). Unpublished report (pursuant to contract #282–77–0219–MS) to the National Institute of Mental Health, Bethesda, MD.

Raghunathan, T. E., Rosenthal, R., & Rubin, D. B. (1996). Comparing correlated but nonoverlapping correlations. *Psychological Methods, 1,* 178–183.

Reichardt, C. S. (1979). The statistical analysis of the nonequivalent group designs. In T. D. Cook & D. T. Campbell, *Quasi-experimenta-*

tion: Design and analysis for field settings (pp. 147–205). Boston: Houghton Mifflin.

Reichardt, C. S. (1985). Reinterpreting Seaver's (1973) study of teacher expectancies as a regression artifact. *Journal of Educational Psychology, 77*, 231–236.

Rogosa, D. R. (1979). Causal models in longitudinal research: Rationale, formulation, and interpretation. In J. R. Nesselroade & P. B. Baltes (Eds.), *Longitudinal research in the study of behavior and development* (pp. 263–301). New York: Academic Press.

Rogosa, D. R. (1980). A critique of cross-lagged correlation. *Psychological Bulletin, 88*, 245–258.

Rogosa, D. R., Brandt, D., & Zimowski, M. (1982). A growth curve approach to the measurement of change. *Psychological Bulletin, 92*, 726–748.

Rogosa, D. R., & Willett, J. B. (1985). Satisfying a simplex structure is simpler than it should be. *Journal of Educational Statistics, 10*, 99–107.

Rosenbaum, P., & Rubin, D. B. (1983). The central role of the propensity score in observational studies for causal effects. *Biometrika, 70*, 41–55.

Rosenthal, R., & Rosnow, R. L. (1991). *Essentials of behavioral research: Methods and data analysis* (2nd ed.). New York: McGraw-Hill.

Rozelle, R. M., & Campbell, D. T. (1969). More plausible rival hypotheses in the cross-lagged panel correlation technique. *Psychological Bulletin, 71*, 74–80.

Rulon, P. J. (1941). Problems of regression. *Harvard Educational Review, 11*, 213–223.

Sapirstein, G. (1995). *The effectiveness of placebos in the treatment of depression: A meta-analysis.* Unpublished doctoral dissertation, University of Connecticut, Storrs.

SAS Institute. (1984). *SAS/ETS users' guide* (Version 5 ed.). Cary, NC: Author.

Simonton, D. K. (1974). *The social psychology of creativity: An archival data analysis.* Unpublished doctoral dissertation, Harvard University.

Simonton, D. K. (1994). *Greatness: Who makes history and why.* New York: Guilford Press.

Smith, G. (1997). Do statistics test scores regress toward the mean? *Chance, 10*, 42–45.

Steiger, J. H. (1980). Tests for comparing elements of a correlation matrix. *Psychological Bulletin, 87*, 245–251.

Stogdill, R. M. (1948). Personal factors associated with leadership: A survey of the literature. *Journal of Personality, 25*, 35–71.

Sutcliffe, J. P. (1980). On the relationship of reliability to statistical power. *Psychological Bulletin, 88*, 509–515.

Swann, W. B., Jr. (1984). Quest for accuracy in person perception: A matter of pragmatics. *Psychological Review, 91*, 457–477.

Taylor, J., & Cuave, K. L. (1994). The sophomore slump among professional baseball players: Real or imagined? *International Journal of Sport Psychology, 25*, 230–239.

Thorn, J., Palmer, P., & Gershman, M. (Eds.). (1997). *Total baseball: The official encyclopedia of major league baseball* (5th ed.). New York: Viking Press.

Trochim, W. M. K. (1984). *Research design for program evaluation.* Beverly Hills, CA: Sage.

Wainer, H. (1991). Adjusting for differential base rates: Lord's paradox again. *Psychological Bulletin, 109*, 147–151.

Warner, R. (1998). *Spectral analysis of time-series data.* New York: Guilford Press.

Whitney, C. W., & Von Korff, M. (1992). Regression toward the mean in treated versus untreated chronic pain. *Pain, 50*, 281–285.

Wilder, J. (1950). The law of initial values. *Psychosomatic Medicine, 12*, 392.

Williams, R. H., & Zimmerman, D. W. (1977). The reliability of difference scores when errors are correlated. *Educational and Psychological Measurement, 77*, 679–689.

Wohlwill, J. F. (1973). *The study of behavioral development.* New York: Academic Press.

Yee, A. H., & Gage, N. L. (1968). Techniques for estimating the source and direction of causal inference in panel data. *Psychological Bulletin, 70*, 115–126.

Zaccaro, S. J., Foti, R. J., & Kenny, D. A. (1991). Self-monitoring and trait-based variance in leadership: An investigation of leader flexibility across multiple group situations. *Journal of Applied Psychology, 76*, 308–315.

Zebrowitz, L. A., Olson, K., & Hoffman, K. (1993). Stability of babyfaceness and attractiveness across the life span. *Journal of Personality and Social Psychology, 64*, 453–466.

Index

Page numbers in boldface denote entries in the Glossary of Terms.